Linux For Beginners

A Comprehensive Guide to Understanding and Mastering Linux

Sarful Hassan

Preface

Welcome to *Linux For Beginners*! This book is designed to provide a clear and concise introduction to Linux, taking you from the basics of understanding the operating system to mastering advanced techniques. Whether you are completely new to Linux or looking to enhance your skills, this book is your companion for learning.

Who This Book Is For
This book is for:

- Absolute beginners who are exploring Linux for the first time.

- IT professionals transitioning to Linux from other operating systems.

- Students and enthusiasts interested in open-source technologies.

- Developers and administrators seeking a structured guide to mastering Linux.

No prior experience with Linux or command-line tools is necessary. We start from the basics and progress gradually to advanced topics.

How This Book Is Organized
The book is structured into 22 chapters, each focusing on a specific aspect of Linux:

- Chapters 1–5 introduce Linux concepts, installation, and the command line.
- Chapters 6–11 cover the file system, shell scripting, and user management.

- Chapters 12–16 delve into disk management, performance monitoring, and security.

- Chapters 17–22 explore advanced topics, including networking, automation, and enterprise use cases.

Each chapter includes step-by-step instructions, examples, and practical exercises to reinforce learning.

What Was Left Out

While this book provides a comprehensive introduction to Linux, certain advanced topics such as kernel programming, advanced networking protocols, and Linux system development are beyond its scope. These topics require specialized resources and experience. However, references for further reading are provided throughout the book.

Release Notes

This is the first edition of *Linux For Beginners*. It reflects the latest advancements in Linux as of the time of writing. Updates and revisions may be included in future editions to address feedback and cover new developments.

Notes on the First Edition

This first edition was crafted to provide a beginner-friendly introduction while balancing depth and breadth. Feedback from readers is highly valued, as it will help refine future editions. If you encounter errors or have suggestions, please don't hesitate to reach out.

MechatronicsLAB Online Learning

For additional resources, tutorials, and interactive learning experiences, visit our online platform:

- **Email:** mechatronicslab@gmail.com
- **Website:** www.mechatronicslab.net

Here, you will find supplemental materials, community forums, and exclusive content to enhance your Linux journey.

How to Contact Us

Your feedback, suggestions, and questions are welcome! Please reach out to us via email or through our website:

- **Email:** mechatronicslab@gmail.com

- **Website:** www.mechatronicslab.net

Acknowledgments for the First Edition

This book would not have been possible without the contributions of the Linux community, whose open-source work inspires countless learners and professionals worldwide. A special thanks to the reviewers, editors, and beta readers who provided invaluable feedback during the development of this book.

Copyright

Disclaimer

Thank you for choosing *Linux For Beginners*. We hope this book inspires you to explore the world of Linux and empowers you to achieve your goals.

Table of Contents

Chapter 1: Introduction to Linux

Overview This chapter provides a friendly and easy-to-understand introduction to Linux, a powerful and versatile open-source operating system. It explains what Linux is, its history, and why it is important. It also highlights Linux's key features, benefits, and uses in everyday life. By the end of this chapter, beginners will feel confident about exploring Linux further.

What is Linux?

Definition and Overview Imagine your computer or smartphone as a busy office. Linux is like the office manager that ensures everything runs smoothly. It organizes all the hardware (like the keyboard, screen, and memory) and helps the software (like apps and browsers) work efficiently. Linux is unique because it's open-source, meaning anyone can look at how it works, suggest improvements, and even customize it.

Linux as an Operating System An operating system is like the brain of your device. It helps your hardware and software communicate and ensures they work together properly. Linux is just one type of operating system, but it's very special because it's free, secure, and reliable.

History and Evolution

Origin of Linux Linux was created in 1991 by Linus Torvalds, a student who wanted to make a free and open operating system. He shared his work online, and soon, people worldwide started helping him improve it. This teamwork made Linux better and more popular.

The Role of Linus Torvalds Linus Torvalds is the person who started Linux. He made it available for everyone to use and improve. Even today, he helps oversee updates to the Linux kernel, which is the core of the operating system.

Milestones in Linux Development

- **1991:** Linus Torvalds shared the first version of Linux.
- **1992:** Linux became open-source, allowing anyone to contribute.
- **1993:** The first Linux distributions (like Debian) were created to make Linux easier to use.
- **2000s:** Companies and developers worldwide adopted Linux for servers, businesses, and personal use.

Key Features and Benefits

Open Source Nature Linux is open-source, meaning it's like a recipe you can read, share, and change as you like. This makes it flexible and encourages innovation.

Security and Stability Linux is less likely to get viruses and crashes. That's why it's trusted for big tasks like running websites and managing bank systems.

Flexibility and Customization Linux can be customized to fit your needs. Whether you want it for a personal computer, a server, or even a small device like a smart light, Linux can be adjusted to work perfectly.

Why Use Linux?

Use Cases in Everyday Life Linux is everywhere! It's in:

- Your Android phone
- Smart TVs
- ATMs and bank systems
- Websites and cloud services like Google

Popular Applications Powered by Linux Big companies like Google, Facebook, and Amazon use Linux. Even supercomputers and space missions rely on it!

Open Source Philosophy

What Does Open Source Mean? Open source is like sharing your work with everyone and letting them improve it. This philosophy makes Linux better every day because of community contributions.

The Role of the Linux Community Linux is supported by a global community of developers, companies, and users. They work together to keep Linux secure, efficient, and up-to-date.

Applications in Everyday Life

Linux in Devices You Use You might not realize it, but Linux is in:

- Android phones
- Smart home devices like Google Nest
- Smart TVs and streaming devices

Linux in Big Businesses Companies use Linux for:

- Running websites and apps
- Managing data and security
- Cloud storage and services

Linux vs. Other Operating Systems

Feature Comparison

Feature	Linux	Windows	macOS
Cost	Free	Paid	Paid
Security	Highly secure	Moderate	Secure
Customization	Extensive	Limited	Limited
Software	Many free apps, but limited proprietary options	Wide variety, including proprietary apps	Focused on proprietary apps
Performance	Efficient on all hardware	Hardware-intensive	Optimized for Apple devices
Support	Community-driven	Official and paid support	Official and limited free support

How Linux Compares to Windows and macOS

- **Cost:** Linux is free, while Windows and macOS cost money.
- **Security:** Linux is less likely to get viruses.
- **Customization:** You can change almost anything in Linux.
- **Software:** While Linux has many free apps, some popular programs like Adobe Photoshop don't work on it yet.

Is Linux Right for You? Linux is great for:

- People who like learning new things
- Developers and tech enthusiasts
- Anyone who wants a secure, free operating system

Chapter 2: Understanding Linux Distributions

Overview This chapter provides a detailed introduction to Linux distributions, often called "distros." It explains what they are, their components, and the differences between popular options like Ubuntu, Fedora, and Arch Linux. Additionally, it covers how to choose the right distribution based on your needs, whether for personal use, professional tasks, or servers. Practical steps for downloading, verifying, and getting started with a Linux distribution are also included, making this chapter a comprehensive guide for beginners and advanced users alike.

What is a Linux Distribution (Distro)?

Definition and Overview A Linux distribution, or "distro," is a version of Linux that combines the Linux kernel with a set of software tools and applications, creating a complete operating system. Each distribution is tailored to specific use cases and user needs, offering unique features, software, and user interfaces.

Components of a Linux Distribution

Component	Description
Linux Kernel	The core of the operating system that manages hardware and system processes.
Package Manager	Tools for installing, updating, and managing software (e.g., APT, YUM, Pacman).
User Interface	Graphical desktop environments or command-line interfaces.
Utilities & Applications	Pre-installed tools like text editors, file managers, and web browsers.

Overview of Popular Distributions

Debian-Based Distributions

Distribution	Key Features
Ubuntu	User-friendly interface, excellent community support, ideal for beginners.
Linux Mint	Polished experience, great for users transitioning from Windows.

Red Hat-Based Distributions

Distribution	Key Features
CentOS	Stable, free, often used for servers, derived from Red Hat Enterprise Linux.
Fedora	Cutting-edge technology, ideal for developers.

Other Popular Distros

Distribution	Key Features
Arch Linux	Highly customizable, minimalist, for advanced users.
SUSE Linux Enterprise	Professional-grade distribution with robust enterprise support.
Manjaro	User-friendly, based on Arch Linux, easier for beginners.

Choosing the Right Linux Distro
Factors to Consider

Factor	Explanation
Use Case	Are you using Linux for personal, professional, or enterprise purposes?
Hardware Compatibility	Ensure the distribution supports your hardware specifications.
Community Support	A strong community can help with troubleshooting and learning.

Recommendations for Beginners

- Ubuntu
- Linux Mint
- Zorin OS

Distributions for Advanced Users

- Arch Linux
- Gentoo
- Slackware

Desktop vs. Server Distributions

Key Differences in Features and Use Cases

Feature	Desktop Distributions	Server Distributions
Purpose	Everyday use with user-friendly features.	Hosting, stability, performance for services.
Resource Requirements	Moderate to high, depends on GUI.	Optimized for low resource usage.
Security	General security.	Enhanced security and long-term support.

Examples of Desktop Distributions

- Ubuntu Desktop
- Pop!_OS

Examples of Server Distributions

- Ubuntu Server
- Red Hat Enterprise Linux

Specific Use Cases

Use Case	Recommended Distros
Development	Fedora, Ubuntu Desktop
Gaming	Pop!_OS, Manjaro
Enterprise	Red Hat Enterprise Linux, SUSE Linux Enterprise

Downloading and Verifying a Linux ISO

How to Download a Distribution ISO File

Step	Description
Visit Website	Go to the official website of the chosen distribution.
Choose ISO	Select the appropriate ISO for your system (e.g., 64-bit).

Importance of Verifying Downloads To ensure the integrity and authenticity of your download, it's crucial to verify the ISO file before installation.

Using Checksums and GPG Keys to Verify Integrity

Verification Method	Description
Checksums	Compare the file's checksum (MD5, SHA256) with the one provided on the official website.
GPG Keys	Use GPG keys to verify that the ISO was signed by the distribution's developers.

Getting Started with a Chosen Distribution

Preparing for Installation

Step	Description
Create Bootable USB	Use tools like Rufus or Etcher to make a bootable USB drive.
Backup Data	Ensure important data is backed up before installation.

Documentation and Community Resources

- Check the official documentation for installation guides and troubleshooting tips.
- Join forums, subreddits, or chat groups dedicated to your chosen distribution for additional support.

Summary By the end of this chapter, you will have a clear understanding of what Linux distributions are, how to choose the right one, and the steps to get started. This chapter caters to absolute beginners and advanced users alike, providing detailed explanations and practical advice to navigate the Linux ecosystem effectively.

Chapter 3: Installing Linux

Overview This chapter is designed to guide absolute beginners through the process of installing Linux. It breaks down each step into simple, clear instructions, ensuring that even first-time users can follow along without confusion. From understanding system requirements to setting up your first Linux environment, this chapter has everything you need to get started. Whether you're installing Linux as your main operating system, alongside Windows, or on a virtual machine, this guide ensures a smooth experience.

By the end of this chapter, you will:

- Understand what Linux needs to run on your computer.
- Prepare your system for installation by creating bootable media.
- Follow step-by-step instructions for installation.
- Configure basic settings to get your system up and running.

System Requirements and Hardware Compatibility

What Does Your Computer Need to Run Linux? To make sure Linux runs smoothly, your computer must meet these basic requirements:

Distribution	Processor	RAM	Disk Space
Ubuntu	Dual-core 2 GHz	4 GB	25 GB
Linux Mint	Dual-core 1 GHz	2 GB	20 GB
Fedora	Dual-core 2 GHz	4 GB	15 GB
Arch Linux	x86_64 compatible	512 MB	2 GB

Checking Your Hardware

- **Processor:** Does your computer support 64-bit? Most modern Linux distributions require this.
- **Memory (RAM):** Ensure you have enough RAM for your chosen distribution. For older computers, lightweight distributions like Lubuntu are a great option.
- **Graphics and Peripherals:** If you have specific devices like printers or Wi-Fi cards, check the distribution's compatibility list to ensure they work.
- Use tools like `inxi` or `hwinfo` to get details about your computer's components.

Preparing for Installation
Step 1: Back Up Your Data
Warning: If you don't back up your data, you risk losing important files during installation.

- Use cloud services (e.g., Google Drive, Dropbox) or external drives to save your files.
- Create a system image if you want to restore your current setup later.

Step 2: Create a Bootable USB Drive
Warning: Be careful to select the correct USB drive to avoid overwriting important data.

1. Download the Linux ISO file from the official website of your chosen distribution.
2. Use tools like Rufus (Windows), Etcher (Linux/macOS), or UNetbootin to create a bootable USB drive.
3. Select the USB drive and follow the tool's instructions to copy the ISO file.

Step 3: Verify Your Download
Note: Verifying the ISO file ensures it hasn't been corrupted or tampered with.

- Download the checksum file from the distribution's website.
- Use tools like `sha256sum` to check the ISO file's integrity.

Installing Linux on Your Machine
Step 1: Start the Installation

Warning: Keep your device plugged into a power source to avoid interruptions.

1. Insert the bootable USB drive and restart your computer.
2. Access the BIOS/UEFI menu (press keys like F2, DEL, or ESC during startup).
3. Set the USB drive as the first boot option and save the changes.
4. Choose "Try Linux" for a live session or "Install Linux" to begin the installation.

Step 2: Follow the Guided Steps

- **Language and Keyboard:** Select your preferred language and keyboard layout.
- **Time Zone:** Choose your location for accurate time settings.
- **Installation Type:**
  - **Automatic:** Ideal for beginners. The system partitions the disk for you.
  - **Manual:** For advanced users who want to customize partitions.
- **Partitions:** If selecting manual, create partitions for:
  - **Root (/):** Main system files.
  - **Home (/home):** Your personal files.
  - **Swap:** Virtual memory.

Step 3: Complete the Installation

- Follow the on-screen instructions to finish setup.
- Remove the USB drive when prompted and restart your computer.

Dual-Booting with Windows

- Shrink your existing Windows partition using Disk Management or GParted.
- Create new partitions for Linux during the installation.
- Install GRUB, the bootloader, to manage your operating systems.

Running Linux on a Virtual Machine

Why Use a Virtual Machine?

- Test Linux without altering your computer.
- Experiment with different distributions.
- Run Linux and another operating system at the same time.

How to Set It Up

1. Install VirtualBox or VMware Workstation.
2. Create a new virtual machine:
   a. Name your virtual machine.
   b. Allocate resources (e.g., 4 GB RAM, 20 GB disk).
   c. Attach the Linux ISO file.
3. Start the virtual machine and follow the installation steps.

Note: Virtual machines may run slower on older hardware. Allocate sufficient resources for smooth performance.

First Boot and Basic Configuration

User Accounts

Note: Use a strong password to protect your system.

- Set up your main user account during installation.
- Decide if you want automatic login or a password prompt at startup.

Choosing a Desktop Environment

- **GNOME:** Modern and sleek.
- **KDE Plasma:** Highly customizable.
- **XFCE:** Lightweight, great for older computers.

Network and Timezone Settings

- Connect to Wi-Fi or Ethernet during setup.
- Set your timezone and region to ensure accurate system settings.

Summary Installing Linux is straightforward when broken down into clear steps. Whether you're a beginner trying Linux for the first time or setting up a dual-boot system, this guide ensures you have all the information needed. With your system up and running, you're ready to explore the world of Linux!

Chapter 4: Navigating the Linux Desktop Environment

Overview This chapter is a detailed, beginner-friendly guide to navigating and customizing Linux desktop environments. It covers the basics of graphical user interfaces (GUIs), introduces popular desktop environments like GNOME, KDE, and XFCE, and provides step-by-step instructions for managing files, customizing the desktop, using workspaces, and troubleshooting. By the end of this chapter, you'll have a solid understanding of how to use and personalize your Linux desktop.

Overview of Graphical User Interfaces (GUIs)

What is a GUI? A GUI, or Graphical User Interface, is a way to interact with your computer using visual elements like windows, icons, and menus instead of typing commands. It makes computers easier to use, especially for beginners, by providing an intuitive and visually rich experience.

Benefits of Using a GUI over the Command Line

- **Ease of Use:** Simple to learn and navigate.
- **Visual Feedback:** Shows the results of your actions immediately.
- **Efficiency:** Enables quick access to files, applications, and settings without remembering commands.

Common Desktop Environments

Introduction to GNOME

- **Features:** Clean, modern design focused on simplicity.
- **Key Tools:** Nautilus (file manager), GNOME Terminal, and a unified search feature.
- **Best For:** General users who prefer a polished, out-of-the-box experience.

KDE: Features and Use Cases

- **Features:** Highly customizable and visually appealing.
- **Key Tools:** Dolphin (file manager), Konsole, and a large collection of apps like KOrganizer.
- **Best For:** Users who want advanced features and full control over their system's look and feel.

XFCE and Other Lightweight Alternatives

- **Features:** Lightweight and fast, designed for older computers or minimal setups.
- **Key Tools:** Thunar (file manager), XFCE Terminal, and simple system settings.
- **Best For:** Users with older hardware or those seeking speed and efficiency.

Tip: Many Linux distributions allow you to try different desktop environments without reinstalling the system. Explore and choose one that suits your preferences!

Managing Files and Folders with File Managers

Using Nautilus in GNOME
- **Overview:** A user-friendly file manager with essential features for beginners.
- **How to Use:**
    - Drag and drop files to move or copy them.
    - Use the search bar to find files quickly.
    - Right-click on files for options like renaming or sharing.

Dolphin File Manager in KDE
- **Overview:** A powerful and flexible file manager.
- **Key Features:**
    - Split view to work with two folders simultaneously.
    - File previews for images and documents.
    - Plugins for advanced features like cloud storage integration.

Thunar for XFCE

- **Overview:** Fast and efficient for basic file operations.
- **Key Features:**
    - Bulk rename tool for organizing multiple files at once.
    - Easy access to external drives and network shares.

Searching for Files and Folders

- **GNOME:** Use the Activities overview or Nautilus search.
- **KDE:** Access the search feature in Dolphin or use KDE's application launcher.
- **XFCE:** Use Thunar's built-in search tool or the application menu.

Tip: Organize your files into folders and use meaningful names to make searching easier.

Customizing Your Desktop
Changing Themes and Icons
- **GNOME:** Go to "Settings" > "Appearance" to switch themes and icons.
- **KDE:** Use "System Settings" > "Global Themes" to download and apply new designs.
- **XFCE:** Navigate to "Settings Manager" > "Appearance" for customization options.

Creating and Managing Shortcuts
- Right-click on the desktop to create shortcuts for frequently used files or applications.
- Drag files or folders onto the desktop for quick access.

Adjusting Screen Resolution and Display Settings
- **GNOME:** Access "Settings" > "Displays" to adjust resolution and scaling.
- **KDE:** Use "Display and Monitor" in System Settings.
- **XFCE:** Open "Settings" > "Display" to make adjustments.

Tip: Experiment with themes and resolutions to find what works best for your preferences and hardware.

Understanding Workspaces and Virtual Desktops

What are Workspaces? Workspaces (or virtual desktops) are separate desktop screens that let you organize your open applications. They help reduce clutter and improve productivity.

Switching Between Workspaces

- **GNOME:** Use the Activities overview or press Super + Arrow Keys.
- **KDE:** Navigate with the desktop pager widget or shortcuts.
- **XFCE:** Use the workspace switcher in the panel.

Managing Multiple Applications with Workspaces

- Assign specific tasks to different workspaces (e.g., one for work apps, another for entertainment).
- Easily switch between tasks without closing windows or losing focus.

Tip: Start with two or three workspaces to get comfortable, then expand as needed.

Basic Troubleshooting in GUI Environments

Resolving Common GUI Issues

- **Frozen Applications:** Open System Monitor or Task Manager to force quit unresponsive apps.
- **Display Problems:** Check and adjust settings in the display configuration menu.

Reverting to Default Desktop Settings

- **GNOME:** Use dconf reset or access reset options in the settings menu.
- **KDE/XFCE:** Restore defaults via the environment's system settings.

Tip: Keep a list of helpful troubleshooting commands and shortcuts handy.

Summary This chapter covers everything you need to navigate and customize a Linux desktop environment. With this guide, you can confidently use GUIs, manage files, personalize your desktop, and troubleshoot common issues. Whether you're exploring GNOME, KDE, or XFCE, this knowledge will make your Linux experience enjoyable and productive.

Chapter 5: Introduction to the Linux Command Line

Overview This chapter is a beginner-friendly guide to the Linux command line. The command line is a text-based way of interacting with your computer that gives you powerful control over your system. This chapter explains the basics of the command line, step-by-step instructions for navigating the file system, using essential commands, and customizing your environment. It is designed to make the Linux command line easy and approachable for new users.

By the end of this chapter, you will:

- Understand the purpose and importance of the command line.
- Learn to navigate the Linux file system with essential commands.
- Master basic file management, permissions, and customization tools.
- Gain confidence in using the terminal as part of your daily Linux experience.

What is the Command Line?

Definition and Purpose The command line is a tool that allows you to interact with your operating system by typing commands. Instead of clicking on icons, you write instructions to perform tasks like managing files, installing programs, or changing settings.

Why is the Command Line Important?

- **Efficiency:** Many tasks can be completed faster using the command line than with a graphical interface.
- **Precision:** Allows you to execute specific commands exactly as needed.
- **Flexibility:** Provides access to advanced features and tools not available in graphical environments.
- **Automation:** Lets you write scripts to handle repetitive tasks automatically.

Real-Life Example: Suppose you want to rename hundreds of files. Using the command line, you can rename them all in seconds with a single command, saving hours of manual work.

Understanding Shells

What is a Shell? A shell is a program that interprets the commands you type and passes them to the operating system. It acts as a bridge between you and the computer.

Types of Shells: Bash, Zsh, and Others

- **Bash (Bourne Again Shell):** The default shell on most Linux systems. Beginner-friendly and versatile.
- **Zsh (Z Shell):** Offers advanced features like auto-suggestions and themes.
- **Fish (Friendly Interactive Shell):** Focuses on simplicity and ease of use with modern features.

How to Check Your Default Shell To see which shell you are using, type:

```
echo $SHELL
```

This command will display the path to your default shell (e.g., /bin/bash).

Tip: You can change your default shell with the chsh command. For example:

```
chsh -s /bin/zsh
```

Opening the Terminal
How to Open the Terminal

- **GNOME:** Press Ctrl + Alt + T or search for "Terminal" in the Activities menu.
- **KDE:** Use Alt + Space to open the application launcher and type "Konsole."
- **XFCE:** Open the application menu and search for "Terminal."

Keyboard Shortcuts for Quick Access

- **Universal Shortcut:** Ctrl + Alt + T (works in most environments).
- **Custom Shortcuts:** You can create custom shortcuts in your system settings.

Warning: Be cautious when running commands as the root user, as mistakes can affect your system.

Navigating the File System

Understanding the Linux Directory Structure Linux organizes files in a hierarchical structure. Here are some key directories:

Directory	Purpose
/	Root directory, the base of the file system.
/home	Stores user home directories (e.g., /home/username).
/etc	Contains configuration files for the system.
/var	Stores variable data, such as logs and temporary files.
/usr	Holds user-installed programs and libraries.

Note: Each directory serves a specific purpose. For example, /home contains user files, while /etc holds system settings.

Essential Navigation Commands

Command	Purpose	Example
pwd	Prints the current directory.	pwd → /home/user
cd	Changes the current directory.	cd Documents → /home/user/Documents
ls	Lists files in a directory.	ls -l → Displays detailed file info.

Tips for Navigation:

- Use the `tab` key to auto-complete file and directory names.
- Use `cd ..` to go up one directory level.

Basic Commands for Beginners

Copying and Moving Files

Command	Purpose	Example
cp	Copies files or directories.	`cp file.txt /home/user/Documents`
mv	Moves or renames files.	`mv file.txt newfile.txt` renames the file.

Tip: Add the `-i` flag (e.g., `cp -i`) to confirm before overwriting files.

Deleting Files and Directories

Command	Purpose	Example
rm	Removes a file.	`rm file.txt` deletes `file.txt`.
rm -r	Removes a directory and its contents.	`rm -r /tmp/test` removes the directory.

Warning: Use the `-i` flag (e.g., `rm -i file.txt`) to confirm deletions and avoid accidental data loss.

Viewing File Contents

Command	Purpose	Example
cat	Displays the entire file content.	`cat file.txt`
more	Views file content one screen at a time.	`more file.txt`
less	Similar to more, but allows backward navigation.	`less file.txt`

Tip: Use `less` for large files to prevent overwhelming your terminal.

Understanding File Permissions

What Are File Permissions? File permissions determine who can read, write, or execute a file.

Permission Levels:

- **Owner:** The user who owns the file.
- **Group:** A group of users with shared access.
- **Others:** Everyone else.

Interpreting the ls -l Output Example output:

```
-rw-r--r-- 1 user group 1024 Jan 1 12:00 file.txt
```

Symbol	Meaning
r	Read permission
w	Write permission
x	Execute permission
-	No permission

Note: In rw-r--r--, the first three symbols (rw-) apply to the owner, the next three (r--) apply to the group, and the last three (r--) apply to others.

Modifying Permissions

Command	Purpose	Example
chmod	Changes file permissions.	chmod 755 file.txt: Sets read, write, execute for owner, and read/execute for others.
chown	Changes file ownership.	chown user:group file.txt: Assigns ownership to user and group.

Tip: Always double-check changes with ls -l after modifying permissions.

Common Command Line Tools

Tool	Purpose	Example
find	Searches for files within a directory structure.	find /home -name file.txt
locate	Quickly finds files using an indexed database.	locate file.txt
grep	Searches for specific text in files.	grep "hello" file.txt
tar	Archives multiple files into one .tar file.	tar -cvf archive.tar file1 file2
gzip	Compresses files to save disk space.	gzip archive.tar

Finding Files

- find [directory] -name [filename]: Searches for files.
  - Example: find /home -name file.txt searches for file.txt in /home.
- locate [filename]: Quickly finds files using an indexed database.
  - Example: locate file.txt lists all paths containing file.txt.

Searching Text in Files

- grep [pattern] [file]: Searches for a pattern in a file.
  - Example: grep "hello" file.txt finds all lines containing "hello."

Compressing Files

- tar -cvf archive.tar [files]: Archives files into a .tar file.
- gzip archive.tar: Compresses the archive to save space.

Tip: Use tar -xvf archive.tar to extract files from a .tar archive.

Customizing Your Command Line Environment

Editing the .bashrc File The `.bashrc` file stores settings for your terminal.

- Add custom aliases to save time.
  - Example: `alias ll='ls -l'` simplifies typing.
- Reload changes with `source ~/.bashrc`.

Changing Your Prompt

- Modify the PS1 variable to personalize your prompt.
  - Example: `PS1='\u@\h:\w$ '` displays your username, hostname, and current directory.

Tip: Test new settings before adding them permanently.

Summary This chapter introduces the Linux command line with step-by-step instructions and practical examples. From navigating the file system to customizing your terminal, you now have the foundational skills to use the command line effectively. With practice, this tool will become an essential part of your Linux journey.

Chapter 6: Linux File System Hierarchy

Overview This chapter is designed to help absolute beginners understand the Linux file system hierarchy. The Linux file system is the backbone of any Linux operating system, organizing data in a structured and predictable manner. By the end of this chapter, you will know the purpose of each key directory, how to navigate the file system, and best practices for managing it efficiently.

By the end of this chapter, you will:

- Understand the Linux file system structure and its importance.
- Learn the functions of key directories like /bin, /home, and /etc.
- Navigate the file system using absolute and relative paths.
- Understand how to handle mount points and hidden files.
- Follow best practices for managing files and directories safely.

What is a File System?

A file system is a method of organizing and storing data on storage devices such as hard drives or SSDs. It provides a framework for creating, reading, modifying, and deleting files and directories.

Why is the Linux File System Important?

- **Organization:** It ensures that files are stored systematically.
- **Accessibility:** Users and applications can easily find and access data.
- **Standardization:** Linux uses the File System Hierarchy Standard (FHS), making it consistent across distributions.

Tip: The Linux file system is like a tree. The root directory (/) is the base, and all other directories branch off from it.

Key Directories in the Linux File System

Directory	Purpose
/bin	Contains essential binary files (e.g., ls, cp, mv).
/home	Stores personal directories for users (e.g., /home/username).
/etc	Holds system configuration files (e.g., /etc/passwd, /etc/hosts).
/var	Stores variable data like logs (/var/log) and temporary files.
/usr	Contains user applications, utilities, and libraries.
/tmp	Temporary files, often cleared on reboot.
/dev	Represents hardware devices (e.g., /dev/sda for disks).
/proc	A virtual file system with real-time process information.
/sys	Contains system and hardware information.

Detailed Examples:

- **/bin:** You can find essential commands here. For example:
  - ls: Lists directory contents.
  - cp: Copies files.
- **/home:** Each user has a personal folder under /home. For instance, /home/john contains John's personal files.
- **/etc:** Configuration files for your system and software. For example:
  - /etc/passwd: Stores user account details.
  - /etc/hosts: Maps IP addresses to hostnames.

Warning: Avoid modifying files in system directories like /etc unless you are certain of their purpose.

Navigating the File System

Commands for Navigation

Command	Purpose	Example
pwd	Prints the current working directory.	pwd → /home/user
cd	Changes the current directory.	cd /etc → Moves to /etc.
ls	Lists directory contents.	ls -l → Detailed file list.

Tips for Beginners:

- Use `cd ..` to move up one directory level.
- Use `tab` for auto-completion of file and directory names.
- Use `ls -lah` to view directory contents with detailed information and human-readable file sizes.

Exploring File System Structure with tree

- **Command:** `tree`
  - Displays a directory structure in a tree-like format.
  - Example:

```
/home/user
├── Documents
├── Downloads
└── Pictures
```

Tip: Install the `tree` command using your package manager if it's not already installed (e.g., `sudo apt install tree`).

Absolute vs. Relative Paths

Path Type	Example	Description
Absolute Path	`/etc/hosts`	Refers to the `hosts` file in `/etc`.
Relative Path	`../Documents/file.txt`	Refers to `file.txt` in the parent `Documents` directory.

Key Differences:

- **Absolute Path:** Always starts from / (root directory).
- **Relative Path:** Starts from your current location.

Practice: Try navigating to /home using both absolute (`cd /home`) and relative paths (e.g., `cd ../home`).

Understanding Mount Points

What are Mount Points? A mount point is a directory where a storage device (e.g., USB drive) is attached to the Linux file system. This allows you to access the device's contents as part of your directory structure.

Command	Purpose	Example
mount	Attaches a device to a directory.	mount /dev/sdb1 /mnt
umount	Detaches the device from the directory.	umount /mnt

Common Mount Points:

Mount Point	Purpose
/mnt	Temporary mount point for storage devices.
/media	Automatically mounts removable media.
/	Root file system, where all directories are mounted.

Warning: Always unmount a device with umount before physically removing it to avoid data loss.

Hidden Files and Directories

What are Hidden Files? Hidden files and directories start with a dot (.). They usually store configuration settings.

Command	Purpose	Example
ls -a	Lists all files, including hidden ones.	ls -a → Shows .bashrc.

Examples of Hidden Files:

- .bashrc: Stores shell settings and aliases.
- .gitconfig: Stores Git configuration.

Tip: Avoid deleting hidden files unless you are sure of their purpose. These files often control application behavior.

Best Practices for File System Management
Keeping the File System Organized
- Create meaningful folder names for your files (e.g., /home/user/Work).
- Regularly clean up unused files and directories.

Avoiding Common Pitfalls
- **Do not use rm -rf carelessly:** This command can delete critical files. Always double-check paths.
- **Backup important files:** Before modifying system files, create backups using tools like cp or rsync.

Monitoring Disk Usage

Command	Purpose	Example
df	Displays available and used disk space.	df -h → Human-readable sizes.
du	Displays disk usage for files and directories.	du -sh /home/user → Shows the size of /home/user.

Tip: Use these commands regularly to ensure you have enough storage space.

Summary The Linux file system hierarchy is the foundation of Linux administration. By understanding key directories, practicing navigation, and following best practices, you can confidently manage your system. Use the commands and tips in this chapter to explore and maintain your Linux file system effectively.

Chapter 7: Managing Software on Linux

Overview This chapter focuses on managing software in Linux using package managers, universal package formats, and graphical tools. It introduces key concepts like installing, updating, and troubleshooting software, and explains best practices for effective software management on Linux.

By the end of this chapter, you will:

- Understand what package managers are and their importance.
- Learn how to install, update, and remove software.
- Use universal package formats like Snap and Flatpak.
- Troubleshoot common software management issues.

What are Package Managers?

Definition and Role of Package Managers A package manager is a tool that automates the process of installing, updating, and removing software. It ensures that all software dependencies are met, making software management easy and efficient.

Advantages of Using Package Managers

- **Efficiency:** Install or update multiple packages with a single command.
- **Dependency Management:** Automatically resolves software dependencies.
- **Security:** Ensures you download software from trusted repositories.

Real-Life Example: Using `apt-get install firefox` installs Firefox along with any additional libraries it requires.

Best Practices:

- Regularly update your package manager's database to ensure access to the latest software versions (`sudo apt-get update`).
- Uninstall unused software to free up disk space and reduce security risks.
- Prefer official repositories for downloads to maintain system integrity.

Popular Linux Package Managers

Package Manager	Supported Distributions	Key Features
APT	Debian-based (Ubuntu)	Simple, widely supported, easy to use.
YUM/DNF	Red Hat-based (Fedora)	Advanced features for enterprise use.
Zypper	openSUSE	Focuses on dependency resolution.
Pacman	Arch Linux	Lightweight and efficient.

Comparing Features:

- **APT:** Best for beginners, available in Ubuntu and Debian.
- **DNF/YUM:** Offers robust support for managing repositories.
- **Zypper:** Excellent for handling complex dependencies.
- **Pacman:** Ideal for advanced users who value speed.

Common Pitfalls:

- Forgetting to run `sudo apt-get update` before installing software can lead to outdated packages.
- Adding untrusted repositories may compromise system security. Always verify sources before adding them.

Installing, Updating, and Removing Software

Using APT for Debian-based Systems APT is the default package manager for Debian-based distributions like Ubuntu.

Command	Purpose	Example
`apt-get install`	Installs a package.	`sudo apt-get install vim`
`apt-get remove`	Removes a package.	`sudo apt-get remove vim`
`apt-get update`	Updates package lists from repositories.	`sudo apt-get update`
`apt-get upgrade`	Installs available updates.	`sudo apt-get upgrade`

Note: Always run `sudo apt-get update` before installing new software to ensure you have the latest package lists.

Commands for Adding, Removing, and Updating Packages

- **Add a Package:** `sudo apt install package-name`
- **Remove a Package:** `sudo apt remove package-name`
- **Upgrade All Packages:** `sudo apt upgrade`

Warning: Removing essential system packages can cause instability. Double-check before running removal commands.

Managing Repositories

What are Software Repositories? Repositories are centralized locations where Linux software packages are stored. They ensure that users download verified and secure software.

Adding and Removing Repositories Safely

Command	Purpose	Example
`sudo add-apt-repository ppa:name`	Adds a new repository.	`sudo add-apt-repository ppa:repository-name`
`sudo add-apt-repository --remove ppa:name`	Removes a repository.	`sudo add-apt-repository --remove ppa:name`
`sudo apt-get update`	Updates package lists from repositories.	`sudo apt-get update`

Note: Only add repositories from trusted sources to avoid installing malicious or unstable software.

Troubleshooting Repository Issues

- Check repository settings in `/etc/apt/sources.list`.
- Use `sudo apt-get update` to refresh repository data.
- Resolve errors like "404 Not Found" by removing outdated repositories.

Warning: Misconfigured repositories can lead to broken package installations. Review repository configurations carefully.

Introduction to Snap and Flatpak

What are Universal Package Formats? Universal package formats like Snap and Flatpak allow software to run on different Linux distributions without modification.

Installing and Managing Snap Packages

Command	Purpose	Example
sudo apt install snapd	Installs Snap package manager.	sudo apt install snapd
sudo snap install	Installs a Snap package.	sudo snap install package-name
snap list	Lists installed Snap packages.	snap list
sudo snap remove	Removes an installed Snap package.	sudo snap remove package-name

Note: Snap packages are self-contained and include all required dependencies, which makes them convenient for cross-distribution compatibility.

Warning: Be mindful of disk space usage when installing multiple Snap packages, as they may consume more space compared to native packages.

Using Flatpak for Application Management

Command	Purpose	Example
sudo apt install flatpak	Installs Flatpak package manager.	sudo apt install flatpak
flatpak remote-add	Adds a Flatpak repository.	flatpak remote-add --if-not-exists flathub https://flathub.org/repo/flathub.flatpakrepo
flatpak install	Installs a Flatpak package.	flatpak install flathub package-name
flatpak list	Lists installed Flatpak packages.	flatpak list
flatpak uninstall	Removes an installed Flatpak package.	flatpak uninstall package-name

Note: Flatpak packages are sandboxed, meaning they run in isolated environments, enhancing security.

Warning: Flatpak applications may require additional runtime libraries, which can increase disk space usage. Always verify available storage before installation.

Advanced Software Management

Using Graphical Tools for Package Management Most Linux distributions provide GUI tools for software management, such as:

- **Ubuntu Software Center** (Ubuntu)
- **Discover** (KDE)
- **Yast** (openSUSE)

These tools are user-friendly and ideal for beginners.

Automating Software Updates

Command	Purpose	Example
`sudo crontab -e`	Opens the cron editor for scheduling.	`sudo crontab -e`
`apt-get update && apt-get upgrade -y`	Updates and upgrades all packages.	Scheduled with `cron` for weekly updates.

Managing Dependencies and Conflicts

Issue	Cause	Solution
Missing dependencies	Required packages are not installed.	Run `sudo apt-get install -f` to fix issues.
Conflicting packages	Two packages require different versions.	Remove conflicting package with `sudo apt-get remove`.

Note: Dependency conflicts occur when two packages require different versions of the same library. Resolving these conflicts promptly prevents issues.

Common Errors and Solutions

Error	Cause	Solution
Broken packages	Interrupted installation or dependency issues	Run `sudo dpkg --configure -a` to reconfigure packages.
Missing dependencies	Required packages are not installed	Use `sudo apt-get install -f` to fix missing dependencies.
Repository errors (e.g., 404)	Outdated or misconfigured repositories	Check `/etc/apt/sources.list` and update repositories.
Cache taking up space	Accumulated package manager cache files	Clear the cache with `sudo apt-get clean`.
Installation failures	Incorrect or missing dependencies	Use `--verbose` with the installation command to debug issues.

Resolving Broken Packages

Issue	Command	Description
Reconfigure packages	`sudo dpkg --configure -a`	Resolves incomplete installations.
Fix dependencies	`sudo apt-get install -f`	Repairs missing or broken dependencies.
Clear package cache	`sudo apt-get clean`	Frees up disk space by removing cached files.

Debugging Installation Failures

Step	Description
Review error messages	Examine terminal output for specific errors.
Search for solutions	Use forums or documentation for troubleshooting.
Enable verbose mode	Add `--verbose` to commands for detailed logs.

Warning: Avoid interrupting package installations to prevent system instability. Use the listed commands to recover if interruptions occur.

Summary Managing software on Linux is straightforward once you understand package managers and universal package formats. By learning how to install, update, and troubleshoot software, you can maintain a secure and efficient system. Use the following appendix for quick reference to the commands covered in this chapter:

Appendix: Key Commands

Task	Command	Example
Update package database	`sudo apt-get update`	`sudo apt-get update`
Install a package	`sudo apt-get install package-name`	`sudo apt-get install vim`
Remove a package	`sudo apt-get remove package-name`	`sudo apt-get remove vim`
Fix dependencies	`sudo apt-get install -f`	`sudo apt-get install -f`
Add a repository	`sudo add-apt-repository ppa:name`	`sudo add-apt-repository ppa:example`
Remove a repository	`sudo add-apt-repository --remove ppa:name`	`sudo add-apt-repository --remove ppa:example`
Clear cache	`sudo apt-get clean`	`sudo apt-get clean`

With these tools and best practices, you can confidently manage software on your Linux system.

Chapter 8: Managing Users and Permissions

Overview This chapter provides a beginner-friendly guide to managing users and permissions in Linux. User management is essential for system administration, allowing you to control who can access resources and perform specific tasks. By understanding user roles, groups, and file permissions, you can maintain a secure and efficient Linux environment.

By the end of this chapter, you will:

- Understand the different types of user accounts.
- Learn how to add, delete, and modify users and groups.
- Master the basics of file permissions and ownership.
- Apply advanced permission settings like Setuid, Setgid, and Sticky Bit.
- Follow best practices for user and permission management.

Understanding User Accounts

What are User Accounts in Linux? User accounts allow individuals to access a Linux system while maintaining separation of personal and system data. Each user has unique credentials and settings.

Types of Users: Root, Regular, and System Users

User Type	Description	Examples
Root User	The superuser with full system access.	`root`
Regular Users	Users with limited privileges.	`john`, `alice`
System Users	Accounts used by system processes and services.	`www-data`, `nobody`

Root vs. Regular Users

- **Root User:**
    - Has unrestricted access to all files and commands.
    - Can perform critical tasks like system updates and configuration changes.
- **Regular Users:**
    - Have limited access, restricted to their home directory and files they own.
    - Cannot modify system-critical files without elevated permissions.

Warning: Avoid using the root account for routine tasks to prevent accidental system changes or data loss.

Note: Create a strong password for the root account and use it sparingly to minimize risks.

Adding, Deleting, and Modifying Users
Adding New Users with adduser and useradd

Command	Purpose	Example
adduser username	Adds a new user with interactive prompts.	sudo adduser john
useradd username	Adds a new user with fewer prompts.	sudo useradd alice

Modifying User Details with usermod

Command	Purpose	Example
usermod -aG groupname username	Adds a user to a group.	sudo usermod -aG sudo john
usermod -l newname oldname	Changes a username.	sudo usermod -l alice newalice

Removing Users Safely with userdel

Command	Purpose	Example
userdel username	Deletes a user account.	sudo userdel john
userdel -r username	Deletes a user and their home directory.	sudo userdel -r john

Note: Use userdel -r carefully, as it permanently removes user data.

Warning: Always double-check the username before deleting an account to avoid unintentional data loss.

Understanding Groups

Purpose of Groups in Linux Groups allow multiple users to share access to files and directories. They simplify permission management for teams and services.

Types of Groups: Primary and Secondary Groups

- **Primary Group:** Assigned to a user by default; usually matches the username.

- **Secondary Groups:** Additional groups a user can belong to for shared access.

Managing Groups

Command	Purpose	Example
groupadd groupname	Creates a new group.	sudo groupadd developers
groupdel groupname	Deletes a group.	sudo groupdel developers
usermod -aG groupname username	Adds a user to a group.	sudo usermod -aG developers john
groups username	Lists groups a user belongs to.	groups john

Note: Ensure users are assigned to appropriate groups to avoid unintentional access restrictions.

Warning: Deleting a group may affect access permissions for all members of that group. Verify before proceeding.

Understanding File Permissions

Permission Types: Read, Write, Execute Permissions determine what actions can be performed on a file or directory.

Symbol	Permission	Description
r	Read	View the file or list directory contents.
w	Write	Modify the file or directory contents.
x	Execute	Run the file or enter the directory.

File Ownership: User, Group, Others Every file has three ownership categories:

- **User:** The file owner.
- **Group:** A group that has access.
- **Others:** All other users on the system.

Advanced Permissions

Using chmod for Permission Changes

- Symbolic mode: chmod u+rwx file.txt
  chmod g+rw file.txt
  chmod o-r file.txt
- Octal mode: chmod 755 file.txt
  chmod 644 file.txt

Changing Ownership with chown

Command	Purpose	Example
`chown user file`	Changes file owner.	`sudo chown john file.txt`
`chown user:group file`	Changes file owner and group.	`sudo chown john:developers file.txt`

Assigning Group Ownership with chgrp

Command	Purpose	Example
`chgrp group file`	Changes group ownership of a file.	`sudo chgrp developers file.txt`

Warning: Ensure permission changes do not inadvertently grant excessive access to sensitive files.

Special Permission Modes
Setuid, Setgid, and Sticky Bit Explained

- **Setuid:** Ensures a program runs with the file owner's privileges.
- **Setgid:** Ensures files created in a directory inherit the group ownership.
- **Sticky Bit:** Prevents users from deleting files they don't own in a shared directory.

Use Cases for Special Permissions

- Setuid: Used in programs like `sudo` to execute tasks with elevated privileges.
- Setgid: Commonly applied to shared team directories.
- Sticky Bit: Ideal for shared directories like `/tmp`.

Examples:

- Apply Setuid: `chmod u+s file`
- Apply Setgid: `chmod g+s directory`
- Apply Sticky Bit: `chmod +t directory`

Warning: Use special permissions cautiously to avoid security risks.

Practical Examples and Common Scenarios

Securing Shared Directories
- Create a shared directory for a team: `mkdir /shared/team`
  `sudo chown :developers /shared/team`
  `sudo chmod 2775 /shared/team`
- Add users to the `developers` group to grant access.

Assigning Permissions for Team Collaboration
- Allow team members to create and edit files: `chmod g+rw /shared/team`
- Prevent unauthorized users from modifying files: `chmod o-rwx /shared/team`

Note: Regularly review shared directory permissions to ensure compliance with security policies.

Best Practices for User and Permission Management
Avoiding the Overuse of Root Privileges
- Use `sudo` for administrative tasks instead of logging in as root.
- Limit root access to prevent accidental system damage.

Regularly Auditing User Accounts and Permissions
- Review user accounts: `cat /etc/passwd`
- Review group memberships: `cat /etc/group`
- Check file permissions: `ls -l /path/to/files`

Tip: Schedule periodic audits to ensure user and permission settings remain secure.

Warning: Inactive accounts should be reviewed and removed to prevent unauthorized access.

Summary Managing users and permissions is critical for Linux system administration. By understanding user roles, file ownership, and permission settings, you can create a secure and efficient environment.

Appendix: Key Commands Summary

Task	Command	Example
Add a new user (interactive)	`adduser username`	`sudo adduser john`
Add a new user (non-interactive)	`useradd username`	`sudo useradd alice`
Modify user details (add to group)	`usermod -aG groupname username`	`sudo usermod -aG sudo john`
Delete a user	`userdel username`	`sudo userdel john`
Delete a user and home directory	`userdel -r username`	`sudo userdel -r john`
Create a new group	`groupadd groupname`	`sudo groupadd developers`
Delete a group	`groupdel groupname`	`sudo groupdel developers`
Add a user to a group	`usermod -aG groupname username`	`sudo usermod -aG developers john`
Change file permissions (symbolic)	`chmod [permissions] file`	`chmod u+rwx file.txt`
Change file permissions (octal)	`chmod [octal] file`	`chmod 755 file.txt`
Change file owner	`chown user file`	`sudo chown john file.txt`
Change file owner and group	`chown user:group file`	`sudo chown john:developers file.txt`
Change group ownership	`chgrp group file`	`sudo chgrp developers file.txt`
Apply Setuid permission	`chmod u+s file`	`chmod u+s /usr/bin/example`

Apply Setgid permission	`chmod g+s directory`	`chmod g+s /shared/team`
Apply Sticky Bit permission	`chmod +t directory`	`chmod +t /shared/team`
List groups for a user	`groups username`	`groups john`
Review user accounts	`cat /etc/passwd`	`cat /etc/passwd`
Review group memberships	`cat /etc/group`	`cat /etc/group`
Check file permissions	`ls -l`	`ls -l /path/to/files`

With these tools and techniques, you can confidently manage users and permissions on your Linux system.

Chapter 9: Networking Basics in Linux

Overview This chapter introduces the fundamentals of networking in Linux, including configuring network settings, managing interfaces, and using essential networking tools. Understanding networking is vital for Linux system administrators and anyone working with Linux systems in connected environments.

By the end of this chapter, you will:

- Understand basic networking concepts.
- Learn to configure IP addresses and network interfaces.
- Use common networking commands and troubleshoot network issues.
- Explore basic firewall configurations and file-sharing protocols.

What is Networking?

Definition and Importance Networking refers to the communication between devices over a network to share data and resources. In Linux, networking enables system updates, remote management, and access to shared resources.

Networking in Linux: An Overview Linux supports a wide range of networking tools and protocols, making it highly versatile for both personal and enterprise-level networking tasks. Common use cases include server management, cloud computing, and file sharing.

Note: Understanding basic networking concepts is crucial for troubleshooting and optimizing system connectivity.

IP Addressing and Subnetting

Understanding IP Addresses An IP address is a unique identifier assigned to devices on a network.

IP Version	Address Format	Example
IPv4	32-bit (e.g., x.x.x.x)	192.168.1.1
IPv6	128-bit (e.g., x:x:x:x)	2001:0db8::1

Introduction to Subnetting Subnetting divides a network into smaller subnetworks to improve efficiency and security. A subnet mask, such as 255.255.255.0, determines the network and host portions of an IP address.

Practical Example for Subnetting

- **Scenario:** You are assigned the IP range 192.168.1.0/24 and need to create four subnets.
- Subnet mask calculation: Divide the 256 addresses into four equal subnets by incrementing the subnet mask to /26.
- Resulting subnets:
  - 192.168.1.0/26 (hosts: 192.168.1.1 to 192.168.1.62)
  - 192.168.1.64/26 (hosts: 192.168.1.65 to 192.168.1.126)

IPv4 vs. IPv6 Basics

- **IPv4:** Widely used but limited to about 4.3 billion addresses.
- **IPv6:** Supports a virtually unlimited number of devices, ensuring future scalability.

Tip: Use ip addr to view your device's IP address and subnet information.

Warning: Misconfigured subnetting can cause devices to lose connectivity. Plan carefully before implementation.

Configuring Network Settings

Setting Up Static IP Addresses To configure a static IP address, edit the network configuration file (e.g., `/etc/network/interfaces`):

```
sudo nano /etc/network/interfaces
```

Example configuration:

```
iface eth0 inet static
    address 192.168.1.100
    netmask 255.255.255.0
    gateway 192.168.1.1
```

Restart the network service to apply changes:

```
sudo systemctl restart networking
```

Configuring Dynamic IP Addresses with DHCP Dynamic IP addresses are automatically assigned by a DHCP server. To enable DHCP, update the configuration file:

iface eth0 inet dhcp

Restart the service:

```
sudo systemctl restart networking
```

Warning: Incorrect configuration can disrupt connectivity. Always verify settings before restarting services.

Managing Network Interfaces

Physical vs. Virtual Interfaces

- **Physical Interfaces:** Represent actual hardware (e.g., eth0, wlan0).
- **Virtual Interfaces:** Software-based interfaces (e.g., lo for localhost, tun0 for VPNs).

Managing Interface Configurations

Command	Purpose	Example
`ifconfig`	Displays or configures network interfaces.	`ifconfig eth0`
`ip addr`	Displays IP address details.	`ip addr show eth0`
`ip link set`	Enables or disables interfaces.	`sudo ip link set eth0 up`

Note: The `ifconfig` command is deprecated but still available in some distributions. Use `ip` for modern systems.

Tip: Use `ip link show` to list all available network interfaces.

Wireless Networking Basics

To connect to a Wi-Fi network:

1. Identify available networks:
   ```
   nmcli dev wifi list
   ```
2. Connect to a network:
   ```
   nmcli dev wifi connect "SSID" password
   "your_password"
   ```
3. Check connection status:
   ```
   nmcli connection show
   ```

Tip: Use `iwconfig` for older systems that do not support `nmcli`.

Warning: Ensure your Wi-Fi password is stored securely and avoid using public networks without encryption.

Common Networking Commands

Command	Purpose	Example
ping	Tests connectivity to a host.	ping google.com
netstat	Views active connections and ports.	netstat -tuln
ss	Modern replacement for netstat.	ss -tuln
traceroute	Diagnoses network paths.	traceroute google.com
nmap	Scans networks for open ports.	nmap 192.168.1.0/24

Tip: Use `ping` to test basic connectivity and `traceroute` for diagnosing routing issues.

Warning: Use tools like `nmap` responsibly to avoid unauthorized scanning.

Firewall Troubleshooting

Scenario: After enabling a firewall, you can no longer SSH into the server.

1. Allow SSH through the firewall: `sudo ufw allow 22/tcp`
2. Check the firewall status: `sudo ufw status verbose`
3. Restart the firewall service: `sudo systemctl restart ufw`

Tip: Always test firewall rules on a separate connection to avoid locking yourself out.

Note: Keep a backup of your firewall rules to restore in case of misconfiguration.

Real-World Applications
Setting Up a Basic Web Server

1. Install Apache:
   `sudo apt install apache2`
2. Start and enable the Apache service:
   `sudo systemctl start apache2`
   `sudo systemctl enable apache2`
3. Allow HTTP and HTTPS traffic through the firewall:
   `sudo ufw allow 80/tcp`
   `sudo ufw allow 443/tcp`
4. Verify the server is running by visiting `http://your server ip` in a browser.

Tip: Combine this with static IP configuration for reliable server accessibility.

File Sharing with Samba

- Install Samba:
  `sudo apt install samba`
- Edit the Samba configuration file to share a directory:
  `sudo nano /etc/samba/smb.conf`
  Add: `[shared]`
      `path = /home/user/shared`
      `read only = no`
- Restart the Samba service: `sudo systemctl restart smbd`

Note: Samba is useful for sharing files between Linux and Windows systems.

Quick Reference for Common Networking Commands

Task	Command	Example
View IP address details	`ip addr`	`ip addr show eth0`
Enable a network interface	`ip link set interface up`	`sudo ip link set eth0 up`
Test network connectivity	`ping hostname`	`ping google.com`
View active connections	`ss -tuln`	`ss -tuln`
Trace a network route	`traceroute hostname`	`traceroute google.com`
Scan a network for devices	`nmap subnet`	`nmap 192.168.1.0/24`
Configure a firewall rule	`ufw allow port/protocol`	`sudo ufw allow 22/tcp`
Restart the network service	`systemctl restart networking`	`sudo systemctl restart networking`

Summary This chapter covered the basics of networking in Linux, including IP addressing, configuring interfaces, wireless networking, and using essential tools like ping, traceroute, and nmap. Practical scenarios such as firewall troubleshooting and setting up a web server provide real-world applications to enhance your understanding. With these skills, you are equipped to manage and troubleshoot Linux networking effectively.

Chapter 10: Working with Processes

Overview This chapter explores processes in Linux, including how to view, manage, and troubleshoot them. Processes are the foundation of any operating system, enabling programs to run and perform tasks. By understanding processes, you can optimize system performance and address common issues.

By the end of this chapter, you will:

- Understand the basics of processes and their states.
- Learn to manage foreground and background processes.
- Use tools to monitor and troubleshoot processes.
- Adjust process priorities to optimize resource allocation.

What are Processes?

Definition and Overview of Processes A process is an instance of a running program. In Linux, each process is assigned a unique Process ID (PID) and runs within its own environment, isolated from other processes.

How Processes Work in Linux

- Linux uses a hierarchical structure for processes, with each process having a parent process (except for `init` or `systemd`, which is the root of all processes).
- Processes can create child processes, which inherit certain properties from their parent.

Note: Use the `ps` command to view processes and their parent-child relationships.

Understanding Process States

State	Description
Running	Actively using the CPU.
Sleeping	Waiting for an event (e.g., I/O operation).
Zombie	Terminated but not yet removed by its parent.

Transition Between States Processes can move between states depending on their activity. For example, a process might sleep while waiting for input and then transition to running when it receives data.

Warning: A system with too many zombie processes may indicate issues with parent processes failing to clean up.

Foreground vs. Background Processes

What are Foreground Processes? Foreground processes are those that run interactively, occupying the terminal until they finish or are stopped.

Running Processes in the Background To run a process in the background, append an & to the command:
```
sleep 60 &
```

Switching Between Foreground and Background Processes
1. Suspend a foreground process: Ctrl+Z
2. Resume it in the background: bg
3. Bring a background process to the foreground: fg

Tip: Use the jobs command to list background jobs.

Viewing Running Processes

Using ps to View Processes
- Basic usage: ps
- Detailed process list: ps aux

Real-Time Monitoring with top and htop
- **top:** Displays a real-time view of system resource usage: top
- **htop:** An enhanced version of top with a user-friendly interface (install it if not available): sudo apt install htop
  htop

Filtering and Sorting Process Information
- Filter processes by name: ps aux | grep process_name
- Sort processes by memory usage in top: Press Shift+M while in the top interface.

Note: Use htop for a more intuitive and colorful interface compared to top.

Managing Processes
Starting and Stopping Processes
- Start a process: `command`

Stop a process gracefully: kill PID

Suspending and Resuming Processes
- Suspend a process: `kill -STOP PID`
- Resume a suspended process: `kill -CONT PID`

Killing Processes with kill and pkill
- Kill a process by PID: `kill PID`
- Kill all processes with a specific name: `pkill process_name`

Warning: Use `kill` and `pkill` cautiously to avoid terminating critical system processes.

Understanding Process Priorities
What are Nice and Renice Values?
- **Nice Value:** Determines the priority of a process. The lower the value, the higher the priority.
- **Range:** -20 (highest priority) to 19 (lowest priority).

Adjusting Process Priorities with nice and renice
- Start a process with a specific priority: `nice -n 10 command`
- Change the priority of a running process: `renice 5 -p PID`

Tip: Only root users can assign negative nice values to increase priority.

Monitoring Resource Usage
CPU and Memory Utilization by Processes
- View resource usage with `top` or `htop`.
- Use `ps` for a snapshot of CPU and memory consumption: `ps aux --sort=-%cpu`
  `ps aux --sort=-%mem`

Identifying Resource-Intensive Processes
- Use `top` or `htop` to identify processes consuming excessive resources.
- Kill resource-hogging processes if necessary: `kill PID`

Warning: Terminating resource-intensive processes without analysis may affect system stability.

Troubleshooting Process Issues

Identifying Stuck or Unresponsive Processes

1. Use ps or top to locate the process.
2. Check its state (e.g., "D" for uninterruptible sleep).
3. Terminate if necessary: kill -9 PID

Debugging Tools for Process Issues

- **strace:** Tracks system calls made by a process: strace -p PID
- **lsof:** Lists files opened by a process: lsof -p PID

Tip: Use strace to debug processes stuck in I/O operations.

Quick Reference for Process Management Commands

Task	Command	Example
View running processes	ps aux	ps aux
Monitor processes in real time	top or htop	top
Kill a process	kill PID	kill 1234
Change process priority	renice value -p PID	renice 10 -p 1234
List open files by process	lsof -p PID	lsof -p 1234
Trace system calls of process	strace -p PID	strace -p 1234

Best Practices for Process Management

1. **Use kill Responsibly:**
   a. Avoid using kill -9 unless absolutely necessary. Always attempt a graceful termination first with kill PID.
   b. Identify critical system processes to avoid accidental termination.

2. **Monitor Regularly:**
   a. Use tools like top or htop to regularly monitor resource usage and identify potential issues early.
   b. Schedule periodic checks for zombie processes and investigate their parent processes.

3. **Optimize Priorities:**
   a. Adjust priorities of resource-intensive processes using `nice` and `renice` to ensure critical tasks get adequate CPU time.
   b. Avoid setting excessively high priorities for non-essential processes.
4. **Log and Audit Processes:**
   a. Use `lsof` and `journalctl` to audit process activity and logs.
   b. Maintain a record of processes consuming high resources to identify patterns over time.
5. **Use Background Processes Wisely:**
   a. Run non-critical tasks in the background to free up terminal resources but monitor their impact on overall system performance.
6. **Educate Users:**
   a. If managing a multi-user system, educate users about responsible process management to avoid unintentional conflicts.

Summary This chapter covered the fundamentals of process management in Linux. You learned how to view, manage, and troubleshoot processes, as well as adjust priorities to optimize resource usage. With these tools and techniques, you can effectively manage processes on your Linux system.

Chapter 11: Introduction to Shell Scripting

Overview This chapter introduces shell scripting, a powerful way to automate repetitive tasks and simplify system administration in Linux. Shell scripts allow users to write sequences of commands in a file, making it easier to manage systems efficiently.

By the end of this chapter, you will:
- Understand the basics of shell scripting and its importance.
- Write and execute basic Bash scripts.
- Use control structures like loops and conditional statements.
- Automate tasks and troubleshoot common script issues.

What is Shell Scripting?

Definition and Importance Shell scripting involves writing scripts in a shell language, such as Bash, to execute commands automatically. It simplifies complex tasks by bundling commands into a reusable format.

Use Cases in System Administration
- Automating backups.
- Managing user accounts and permissions.
- Rotating logs.
- Monitoring system performance.
- Deploying applications.

Note: Shell scripting is a fundamental skill for Linux administrators and power users.

Tip: Start with small, simple scripts and gradually incorporate advanced features as you gain confidence.

Basics of Bash Scripts

Why Bash? Overview of Common Shells
- **Bash (Bourne Again Shell):** Default shell for most Linux distributions, known for its simplicity and flexibility.
- **Other Shells:**
  - **Zsh:** Enhanced features and customization.
  - **Fish:** User-friendly syntax and interactive capabilities.

Understanding Script Syntax and Structure

- A shell script typically starts with a shebang (`#!/bin/bash`), which specifies the interpreter.
- Commands are written line by line and executed sequentially.

Example Script:

```
#!/bin/bash
# My first script
echo "Hello, World!"
```

Tip: Use meaningful comments (lines starting with #) to explain the script's functionality.

Warning: Ensure your scripts are error-free, as mistakes can impact your system.

Writing Your First Script
Creating a Simple Script

1. Open a text editor:
   ```
   nano myscript.sh
   ```
2. Add the following content:
   ```
   #!/bin/bash
   echo "This is my first script."
   ```
3. Save and exit the editor.

Adding Comments for Readability

- Use # to add comments: `# This script prints a welcome message`
   ```
   echo "Welcome to shell scripting!"
   ```

Tip: Comments improve readability and help others understand your script.

Using echo and Variables
Displaying Output with echo

- Basic usage: `echo "Hello, Linux!"`
- Use escape characters for formatting: `echo -e "Line1\nLine2"`

Defining and Using Variables

- Define a variable: `name="John"`
- Use the variable: `echo "Hello, $name"`
- Read user input into a variable:
  ```
  read -p "Enter your name: " name
  echo "Hello, $name"
  ```

Environment vs. User-Defined Variables

- **Environment Variables:** Predefined by the system (e.g., $HOME, $PATH).
- **User-Defined Variables:** Created and used within scripts.

Note: Variable names are case-sensitive. Use uppercase for environment variables and lowercase for user-defined variables to avoid conflicts.

Making Scripts Executable

File Permissions for Scripts Scripts need execute permissions to run. Check permissions using `ls -l`:
```
ls -l myscript.sh
```

Using chmod +x to Enable Execution Grant execute permissions:
```
chmod +x myscript.sh
```

Run the script:
```
./myscript.sh
```

Warning: Always verify scripts before making them executable to prevent unintended actions.

Control Structures in Shell Scripts

Using if-else Statements

- Syntax:
  ```
  if [ condition ]; then
      # Commands
  else
      # Commands
  fi
  ```

- Example:
```
if [ "$1" == "admin" ]; then
    echo "Welcome, admin!"
else
    echo "Access denied."
fi
```
Tip: Use [[...]] for advanced string and pattern matching.

Looping with for and while Loops
- **for Loop:** `for i in 1 2 3; do`
  ```
      echo "Number: $i"
  done
  ```
- **while Loop:** `count=1`
  ```
  while [ $count -le 3 ]; do
      echo "Count: $count"
      ((count++))
  done
  ```

Case Statements for Multi-Condition Handling
- Syntax:

```
case                            "$1"                            in
   start)
      echo                "Starting                    service..."
      ;;
   stop)
      echo                "Stopping                    service..."
      ;;
   *)
      echo          "Usage:          $0          {start|stop}"
      ;;
esac
```

Tip: Use case for cleaner handling of multiple conditions.

Automating Tasks with Scripts

Examples of Automation: Backups, Log Rotation

- **Backup Script:** `#!/bin/bash`
  ```
  tar -czf backup.tar.gz /path/to/directory
  echo "Backup completed."
  ```

- **Log Rotation:** `mv logfile.log logfile_$(date +%F).log`
  `echo "Log rotated."`

Scheduling Scripts with Cron

- Edit the cron table: `crontab -e`
- Add a schedule: `0 2 * * * /path/to/script.sh`
  (Runs the script daily at 2 AM.)

Tip: Use `crontab -l` to list scheduled tasks.

Warning: Ensure cron jobs point to valid scripts to avoid errors.

Debugging Shell Scripts

Common Errors and How to Fix Them

- **Syntax Errors:** Check for missing `fi` or `done` in control structures.
- **Permission Issues:** Ensure the script is executable with `chmod +x`.
- **Variable Errors:** Verify variable names and ensure they are correctly referenced.

Using set -x and set -e for Debugging

- **Enable Debugging:** `set -x`
- **Stop on Errors:** `set -e`
- Add these at the beginning of your script to debug effectively.

Tip: Run scripts in a test environment before deploying them in production.

Example Debugging Session:

#!/bin/bash

set   -x

Debugging   example

file="/tmp/example.txt"

if   [-f   "$file"   ];   then

   echo   "File   exists."

else

echo   "File   does   not   exist."

fi

Quick Reference for Shell Scripting Commands

Task	Command	Example
Display output	`echo "message"`	`echo "Hello, Linux!"`
Define a variable	`variable=value`	`name="John"`
Make a script executable	`chmod +x script.sh`	`chmod +x myscript.sh`
Run a script	`./script.sh`	`./myscript.sh`
Schedule a script with Cron	`crontab -e`	`0 2 * * * /path/to/script.sh`
Debug a script	`set -x` or `set -e`	Add `set -x` in the script header

Summary This chapter covered the basics of shell scripting, including writing and executing scripts, using variables, and incorporating control structures like loops and conditionals. By automating tasks with scripts, you can simplify system administration and improve efficiency. Use the examples and tools provided to start building your own shell scripts and troubleshooting effectively.

Chapter 12: Disk Management and Storage

Overview This chapter introduces the essential concepts and tools for managing disks and storage in Linux. Disk management is crucial for maintaining system performance, ensuring data integrity, and optimizing storage usage.

By the end of this chapter, you will:

- Understand disk management and its role in Linux systems.
- Learn to create, format, and mount partitions.
- Monitor disk usage and performance.
- Configure swap space and use Logical Volume Management (LVM).
- Follow best practices for effective disk management.

Understanding Disk Management

What is Disk Management? Disk management involves organizing and maintaining storage devices, including hard drives, SSDs, and USB drives, to ensure optimal performance and reliability.

Role in Linux Systems

- **Storage Allocation:** Managing how data is stored and retrieved.
- **System Performance:** Ensuring efficient disk utilization.
- **Data Security:** Preventing data loss through backups and monitoring.

Note: Proper disk management is critical for both personal and enterprise Linux systems.

Understanding Partitions and File Systems

Types of Partitions: Primary, Extended, Logical

- **Primary Partition:** Directly accessible by the system; limited to four per drive.
- **Extended Partition:** A special partition that holds logical partitions, bypassing the four-partition limit.
- **Logical Partition:** Resides within an extended partition and is used for additional storage.

Common File Systems: ext4, NTFS, FAT32

- **ext4:** Default for most Linux distributions, offering journaling and reliability.
- **NTFS:** Commonly used in Windows systems; supported in Linux for compatibility.
- **FAT32:** Used for external drives and devices; compatible across platforms but with limitations (e.g., file size).

Differences Between File Systems

File System	Max File Size	Journaling	Common Use Cases
ext4	16 TB	Yes	Linux system drives
NTFS	16 EB	Yes	Windows drives, external HDDs
FAT32	4 GB	No	USB drives, SD cards

Tip: Choose a file system based on compatibility and performance requirements.

Managing Disk Space
Checking Disk Usage with df
- View overall disk usage: `df -h`

Analyzing Directory Sizes with du
- Check the size of a directory: `du -sh /path/to/directory`
- Display sizes of all subdirectories: `du -h /path/to/directory`

Cleaning Up Unnecessary Files
- Locate large files: `find / -size +1G`
- Remove unused packages: `sudo apt autoremove`

Warning: Use caution when deleting files. Always back up critical data.

Tip: Regularly monitor disk usage with df and du to prevent running out of space unexpectedly.

Creating and Managing Partitions
Tools for Partitioning: fdisk, parted
- **fdisk:** Command-line utility for partition management. `sudo fdisk /dev/sdX`
- **parted:** Advanced partitioning tool supporting large disks. `sudo parted /dev/sdX`

Steps for Creating Partitions

1. Launch the partitioning tool (e.g., fdisk).
2. Create a new partition: n   # New partition
3. Write changes to the disk: w   # Write changes

Example: Using fdisk to Create a Partition

```
sudo fdisk /dev/sdX
Command (m for help): n
Partition type: primary (p) or extended (e)? p
Partition number (1-4): 1
First sector: [Press Enter for default]
Last sector: [Press Enter for default]
Command (m for help): w
```

Viewing Partition Tables

- Display partition details: lsblk

```
sudo fdisk -l
```

Tip: Always double-check the partition table before writing changes.

Real-World Scenarios

Setting Up a Dual-Boot System

1. Backup existing data before proceeding.
2. Use gparted to resize an existing partition and create space for Linux.
3. Install Linux on the new partition and configure the bootloader (e.g., GRUB) to manage both operating systems.
4. Verify both systems boot correctly after installation.

Setting Up a Dedicated Data Partition

1. Create a partition using fdisk or parted.
2. Format the partition: sudo mkfs.ext4 /dev/sdX1
3. Add the partition to /etc/fstab for automatic mounting:
   /dev/sdX1 /mnt/data ext4 defaults 0 2

Tip: Use dedicated partitions for data to separate it from the OS and simplify upgrades.

Formatting and Mounting Drives

Formatting Partitions with mkfs

- Format as ext4: `sudo mkfs.ext4 /dev/sdX1`
- Format as FAT32: `sudo mkfs.vfat /dev/sdX1`

Supported File Systems in Linux

File System	Command to Format
ext4	`sudo mkfs.ext4 /dev/sdX1`
NTFS	`sudo mkfs.ntfs /dev/sdX1`
FAT32	`sudo mkfs.vfat /dev/sdX1`

Mounting and Unmounting Drives

- Mount a drive: `sudo mount /dev/sdX1 /mnt`
- Unmount a drive: `sudo umount /mnt`

Understanding and Configuring /etc/fstab

- Add a drive to `/etc/fstab` for automatic mounting: `/dev/sdX1 /mnt ext4 defaults 0 2`
- Test the configuration: `sudo mount -a`

Warning: Incorrect `/etc/fstab` entries can prevent the system from booting.

Tip: Use descriptive mount points (e.g., `/mnt/backup`) to organize mounted drives effectively.

Troubleshooting Disk Issues

Unrecognized Partitions

- Check partition information: `sudo fdisk -l`
- Re-scan partitions: `sudo partprobe`

Failed Mounts

- Verify `/etc/fstab` entries: `sudo nano /etc/fstab`
- Test manual mounting: `sudo mount /dev/sdX1 /mnt`

Corrupted File Systems

- Repair a file system: `sudo fsck /dev/sdX1`

Tip: Always back up data before attempting repairs.

Common Errors:

- **Error:** "Device is busy."
  - **Solution:** Check processes using the device: `lsof | grep /mnt`
  - Kill the process if safe to do so.

Command Comparison Table

Tool	Purpose	Example Command
fdisk	Partition management	`sudo fdisk /dev/sdX`
parted	Advanced partitioning	`sudo parted /dev/sdX`
lsblk	View disk and partition info	`lsblk`
mkfs	Format partitions	`sudo mkfs.ext4 /dev/sdX1`
mount	Mount partitions manually	`sudo mount /dev/sdX1 /mnt`
df	Check overall disk usage	`df -h`
du	Analyze directory sizes	`du -sh /path/to/directory`
fsck	Repair file systems	`sudo fsck /dev/sdX1`
iotop	Monitor disk I/O	`sudo iotop`

Best Practices for Disk Management

1. **Regular Backups of Critical Data:** Use tools like `rsync` or `tar` for backups.
2. **Monitor Disk Health and Performance:** Use `smartctl` to check disk health.
3. **Ensure Sufficient Free Space:** Maintain at least 20% free space on critical partitions.
4. **Document Changes:** Keep records of partitioning, formatting, and mount points.
5. **Test New Configurations:** Always test mounting and formatting changes on non-critical data before deploying system-wide.

Chapter 13: System Monitoring and Performance

Overview This chapter introduces the essential concepts and tools for monitoring and optimizing system performance in Linux. Proper monitoring helps maintain stability, identify bottlenecks, and ensure efficient resource usage.

By the end of this chapter, you will:

- Understand the importance of system monitoring.
- Learn to use tools for monitoring CPU, memory, disk, and network performance.
- Manage system logs and automate monitoring tasks.
- Optimize performance through analysis and troubleshooting.

Understanding System Monitoring

What is System Monitoring? System monitoring involves observing system resource usage, analyzing performance metrics, and ensuring the system operates smoothly and efficiently.

Key Metrics to Monitor

- **CPU Usage:** Tracks processor activity and workload.
- **Memory Usage:** Monitors RAM and swap utilization.
- **Disk I/O:** Analyzes read/write activity and potential bottlenecks.
- **Network Traffic:** Observes data flow and network performance.

Importance of System Monitoring

- **Proactive Maintenance:** Prevents downtime by identifying issues early.
- **Performance Optimization:** Ensures resources are allocated efficiently.
- **Capacity Planning:** Prepares for future resource needs.

Tip: Regular monitoring helps prevent system failures and improves overall reliability.

Tools for System Monitoring

Built-in Tools

- **top:** Displays real-time process and resource usage.
- **df/du:** Analyzes disk space usage.
- **free:** Provides memory usage statistics.
- **iostat:** Monitors CPU and disk I/O.

Third-Party Tools

- **htop:** Enhanced version of top with interactive features.
- **iotop:** Monitors real-time disk I/O.
- **iftop:** Analyzes network traffic in real-time.
- **nload:** Monitors incoming and outgoing network bandwidth.

Command Comparison Table

Tool	Purpose	Example Command
top	Monitor real-time processes	top
htop	Enhanced process monitoring	htop
iotop	Monitor disk I/O	iotop
iftop	Monitor network traffic	iftop
nload	View bandwidth usage	nload
df	Check overall disk usage	df -h
du	Analyze directory sizes	du -sh /path/to/dir

Tip: Use a combination of tools for a comprehensive view of system performance.

Monitoring CPU Usage

Using top and htop

- Launch top:

top

- ○ **Key Metrics:**
  - ▪ **PID:** Process ID.
  - ▪ **USER:** Process owner.
  - ▪ **%CPU:** CPU usage percentage.
  - ▪ **%MEM:** Memory usage percentage.
- Install and launch htop:

sudo apt install htop
htop

- o **Features:**
  - Color-coded resource usage.
  - Interactive process management (e.g., killing processes).
  - Search and filter processes using F3.

Using mpstat for Detailed Insights

- Install and run mpstat: `sudo apt install sysstat mpstat -P ALL`
  - o **Metrics:**
    - **%user:** Time spent on user processes.
    - **%iowait:** Time spent waiting for I/O operations.

Practical Scenario:

- **Problem:** System is slow, and CPU usage is high.
- **Solution:** Use `top` to identify the process consuming the most CPU and take action (e.g., kill or optimize the process).

Tip: High `%iowait` values may indicate disk-related bottlenecks.

Monitoring Memory Usage

Tools for Monitoring Memory

- Use `free` to view memory and swap usage: `free -h`
- Monitor memory usage with `htop` or `top`.

Identifying Memory Bottlenecks

- Find memory-intensive processes: `ps aux --sort=-%mem | head`

Managing Swap Usage

- Check swap usage: `swapon --show`
- Add temporary swap if necessary:
  ```
  sudo fallocate -l 1G /swapfile
  sudo chmod 600 /swapfile
  sudo mkswap /swapfile
  sudo swapon /swapfile
  ```

Tip: Regularly monitor memory usage to prevent system slowdowns.

Disk and I/O Monitoring
Analyzing Disk Usage with df and du
- Check overall disk usage with df: `df -h`
- Analyze specific directory sizes with du: `du -sh /path/to/directory`

Monitoring Disk I/O with iotop
- Install and use `iotop`: `sudo apt install iotop`
  `sudo iotop`
  - Identifies processes causing high disk activity.

Practical Scenario:
- **Problem:** Disk usage is high, and the system is slow.
- **Solution:** Use `iotop` to identify processes causing high I/O activity and optimize them.

Tip: Use `iotop` during peak load times to identify disk-intensive processes.

Network Performance Monitoring
Analyzing Network Traffic with iftop and nload
- Install and run `iftop` for real-time bandwidth monitoring:
  `sudo apt install iftop`
  `sudo iftop`
- Use `nload` for a visual representation of network traffic:
  `sudo apt install nload`
  `nload`

Identifying Network Bottlenecks
- View active network connections: `ss -tuln`
- Analyze bandwidth usage per connection using `iftop`.

Practical Scenario:
- **Problem:** Slow internet speed.
- **Solution:** Use `iftop` to identify the source of high bandwidth usage.

Tip: High traffic from unknown IPs may indicate potential security issues.

Log Management
Understanding System Logs
- Key log directories:
  - `/var/log/syslog`: General system logs.
  - `/var/log/auth.log`: Authentication logs.

Using journalctl for Logs
- View recent logs: `journalctl -xe`
- Filter logs by time: `journalctl --since "1 hour ago"`

Practical Scenario:
- **Problem:** Application crashes frequently.
- **Solution:** Check logs in `/var/log` or use `journalctl` to identify the cause of the crash.

Tip: Review logs regularly to identify unusual activity.

Performance Optimization
Identifying and Resolving Bottlenecks
1. Use `top` or `htop` to identify resource-intensive processes.
2. Terminate unresponsive processes: `kill -9 PID`
3. Monitor disk and network performance with `iotop` and `iftop`.

Best Practices for Resource Allocation
- Use `ulimit` to limit resource usage per user: `ulimit -u 100`
- Employ `cgroups` for advanced resource control.

Tip: Regular optimization ensures better system stability and performance.

Automation and Alerts
Setting Up Alerts for Critical Resource Usage
- Schedule resource checks with `cron`: `*/5 * * * * free -h >> /var/log/memory.log`
- Install and configure `monit` for automated alerts:
  ```
  sudo apt install monit
  sudo monit status
  ```

Automating Monitoring with Scripts

- Example script for disk usage monitoring:

```bash
#!/bin/bash
THRESHOLD=80
USAGE=$(df -h / | grep / | awk '{print $5}' | sed 's/%//')
if [ "$USAGE" -gt "$THRESHOLD" ]; then
    echo "Disk usage is above $THRESHOLD%" | mail -s "Disk Alert" admin@example.com
fi
```

Tip: Automating monitoring tasks reduces manual overhead and ensures faster issue detection.

Best Practices for System Monitoring

1. **Regularly Monitor Resources:** Schedule frequent checks for CPU, memory, and disk usage.
2. **Document Issues:** Maintain a log of performance issues and their resolutions.
3. **Automate Alerts:** Set up alerts to notify you of critical conditions immediately.
4. **Use Logs Effectively:** Review logs regularly to detect and resolve potential issues early.
5. **Combine Tools:** Use different monitoring tools together to gain a comprehensive view of system health.

Tip: Combining automated monitoring with manual checks ensures comprehensive system health management.

Summary This chapter covered tools and techniques for system monitoring and performance optimization in Linux. By understanding and managing CPU, memory, disk, and network resources, you can maintain system stability and prevent performance bottlenecks. Automation and alerts further enhance your ability to manage resources effectively.

Chapter 14: Basic Networking Services

Overview This chapter introduces essential networking services in Linux, including setting up web servers, configuring remote access, managing file transfers, and handling DNS services. These are critical for administrators and users who need to establish and maintain network functionality.

By the end of this chapter, you will:
- Set up and configure web servers.
- Configure SSH for secure remote access.
- Manage FTP services for file transfers.
- Understand and configure DNS services.
- Troubleshoot common networking issues.

Setting Up a Simple Web Server

Overview of Web Servers Web servers deliver content to users over the internet or a local network. Commonly used web servers include Apache and Nginx.

Installing Apache for Basic Web Hosting

1. Install Apache:
   ```
   sudo apt update
   sudo apt install apache2
   ```
2. Start and enable the Apache service:
   ```
   sudo systemctl start apache2
   sudo systemctl enable apache2
   ```
3. Verify the setup by visiting http://your_server_ip in a browser.

Note: Ensure that port 80 is open in the firewall to allow HTTP traffic.

Warning: Misconfigured web servers can expose sensitive data. Regularly audit configurations and apply security patches.

Setting Up Nginx for Advanced Configurations

1. Install Nginx: `sudo apt update`
   ```
   sudo apt install nginx
   ```
2. Start and enable Nginx: `sudo systemctl start nginx`
   ```
   sudo systemctl enable nginx
   ```

3. Configure Nginx for a custom site:
```
sudo nano /etc/nginx/sites-available/example.com
```
Add: `server {`
```
    listen 80;
    server_name example.com;
    root /var/www/example.com;
    index index.html;
}
```
4. Enable the configuration:
```
sudo ln -s /etc/nginx/sites-available/example.com
/etc/nginx/sites-enabled/
sudo nginx -t
sudo systemctl reload nginx
```

Real-World Scenario:
- Set up a small business website using Nginx and secure it with HTTPS using Let's Encrypt.

Tip: Use Apache for simpler setups and Nginx for high-performance and load-balancing requirements.

Configuring SSH for Remote Access

What is SSH? SSH (Secure Shell) provides secure, encrypted remote access to Linux systems. It is commonly used for remote server management.

Installing and Enabling SSH on Linux

1. Install the OpenSSH server:
```
sudo apt update
sudo apt install openssh-server
```

2. Start and enable the SSH service:
```
sudo systemctl start ssh
sudo systemctl enable ssh
```

3. Verify the SSH service:
```
sudo systemctl status ssh
```

Configuring SSH for Secure Connections

- Edit the SSH configuration file: `sudo nano /etc/ssh/sshd_config`
  Key settings:
    - Disable root login: `PermitRootLogin no`
    - Change the default port (optional): `Port 2222`
- Restart the SSH service: `sudo systemctl restart ssh`

Warning: Changing the default SSH port can reduce automated attacks but requires updating firewall rules and documentation.

Using Key-Based Authentication

1. Generate an SSH key pair on the client machine:
   `ssh-keygen -t rsa -b 4096`

2. Copy the public key to the server:
   `ssh-copy-id user@server_ip`

3. Verify key-based login: `ssh user@server_ip`

Practical Scenario:

- Set up SSH access for multiple users in a team, restricting access to specific directories for each user.

Tip: Key-based authentication is more secure than password-based login.

Setting Up FTP for File Transfers

Understanding FTP Protocol FTP (File Transfer Protocol) allows transferring files between systems. While basic FTP lacks encryption, secure versions like FTPS or SFTP are recommended.

Installing and Configuring an FTP Server

1. Install vsftpd (Very Secure FTP Daemon):
   ```
   sudo apt update
   sudo apt install vsftpd
   ```
2. Edit the configuration file:
   `sudo nano /etc/vsftpd.conf`
   Key settings:
    a. Allow local users: `local_enable=YES`
    b. Enable file uploads: `write_enable=YES`

3. Restart the FTP service: `sudo systemctl restart vsftpd`

Managing FTP Users and Permissions

- Add a new FTP user:
  ```
  sudo adduser ftpuser
  ```
- Set directory permissions:
  ```
  sudo chown ftpuser:ftpuser /home/ftpuser
  ```

Securing FTP Connections with TLS

1. Generate an SSL certificate:
   ```
   sudo openssl req -x509 -nodes -days 365 -newkey
   rsa:2048 -keyout /etc/ssl/private/vsftpd.key -out
   /etc/ssl/certs/vsftpd.crt
   ```
2. Enable TLS in /etc/vsftpd.conf: `ssl_enable=YES`
   `rsa_cert_file=/etc/ssl/certs/vsftpd.crt`
   `rsa_private_key_file=/etc/ssl/private/vsftpd.key`
3. Restart the FTP service: `sudo systemctl restart vsftpd`

Real-World Scenario:

- Use SFTP to securely transfer sensitive company files between locations.

Note: Traditional FTP transmits data in plain text. Always use SFTP or FTPS for secure file transfers.

Managing DNS Services

Basics of Domain Name System (DNS) DNS translates domain names (e.g., example.com) into IP addresses. It is essential for accessing websites and services over the internet.

Configuring DNS Records for a Domain

- Common DNS record types:
  - **A Record:** Maps a domain to an IP address.
  - **CNAME Record:** Creates an alias for another domain.
  - **MX Record:** Specifies mail servers for a domain.

Installing and Managing a DNS Server

1. Install BIND (Berkeley Internet Name Domain):
   ```
   sudo apt update
   sudo apt install bind9
   ```

2. Configure the DNS zone file:

```
sudo nano /etc/bind/db.example.com
```

Example zone file:

```
$TTL 86400
@ IN SOA ns1.example.com. admin.example.com. (
    1 ; Serial
    604800 ; Refresh
    86400 ; Retry
    2419200 ; Expire
    604800 ) ; Negative Cache TTL
@ IN NS ns1.example.com.
ns1 IN A 192.168.1.1
www IN A 192.168.1.2
```

3. Restart the BIND service:

```
sudo systemctl restart bind9
```

Practical Scenario:

- Configure a DNS server for a company intranet, resolving internal hostnames to private IPs.

Warning: Misconfigured DNS records can lead to service interruptions. Double-check configurations before applying changes.

Tip: Use online DNS testing tools to verify your configuration.

Troubleshooting Networking Issues

Diagnosing Common Connectivity Problems

- Check network interfaces: `ip addr`
- Test connectivity: `ping google.com`

Tools for Network Troubleshooting

- **traceroute:** Tracks the route packets take: `traceroute google.com`
- **netstat/ss:** Displays active network connections: `ss -tuln`

Checking Firewall and Port Configurations

- View firewall rules: `sudo ufw status`
- Allow a specific port: `sudo ufw allow 80/tcp`
- Reload the firewall: `sudo ufw reload`

Real-World Scenario:

- Diagnose and resolve a server's inability to access the internet due to misconfigured firewall rules.

Note: Always test connectivity from both the client and server sides to pinpoint the issue accurately.

Tip: Always verify open ports to ensure security.

Best Practices for Networking Services

1. **Use Secure Protocols:** Prefer SFTP and HTTPS over FTP and HTTP.
2. **Restrict Access:** Limit access to services by IP or user.
3. **Monitor Logs:** Regularly review logs for unusual activity.
4. **Keep Services Updated:** Ensure all networking services are updated to patch vulnerabilities.
5. **Test Configurations:** Use test environments before deploying changes to production.

Tip: Regular audits of networking configurations improve security and reliability.

Summary This chapter covered essential networking services in Linux, including web servers, SSH, FTP, and DNS. By understanding and configuring these services, you can establish secure and efficient network functionality. Troubleshooting tools and best practices further ensure reliable and optimized operations.

Chapter 15: Backups and Data Recovery

Overview Backups and data recovery are vital for ensuring data integrity and minimizing downtime in case of failures or accidental data loss. This chapter covers backup strategies, tools for creating and restoring backups, and methods for recovering lost data.

By the end of this chapter, you will:

- Understand the importance of backups.
- Learn about various backup strategies and tools.
- Automate backup processes.
- Recover lost data and test backup restorations.

Importance of Backups

Why Backups are Essential

- Protects against data loss due to hardware failures, accidental deletions, or cyberattacks.
- Ensures business continuity by minimizing downtime.
- Enables quick recovery of critical files and systems.

Consequences of Data Loss

- Permanent loss of important files and data.
- Downtime resulting in lost productivity or revenue.
- Potential legal or regulatory implications for non-compliance.

Best Practices for Data Backup

Scheduling Regular Backups

- Use a consistent schedule based on the criticality of the data.
- Example: Daily incremental backups and weekly full backups.

Choosing the Right Backup Strategy

Strategy	Description	Pros	Cons
Full Backup	Copies all data.	Easy to restore.	Requires more storage.
Incremental	Backs up changes since the last backup.	Saves storage and time.	Slower to restore.
Differential	Backs up changes since the last full backup.	Balanced approach.	Requires more storage than incremental.

Ensuring Backup Integrity

- Verify backups using checksums or built-in validation tools.
- Regularly test backups by performing restorations.

Warning: Unverified backups can fail when needed most. Always test backup integrity.

Real-World Scenario:

- A business uses full weekly backups with daily incremental backups to minimize storage costs while ensuring quick recovery.

Using Tools for Backup

Overview of Popular Backup Tools

- **rsync:** Efficient file synchronization and transfer.
- **tar:** Archives and compresses files.
- **Third-Party Solutions:** Tools like Bacula, Duplicati, and Timeshift for advanced needs.

Using rsync for Efficient File Sync

1. Install rsync: `sudo apt install rsync`
2. Sync a directory: `rsync -av /source/directory /backup/directory`
3. Use SSH for remote backups: `rsync -avz /source/directory user@remote_host:/backup/directory`

Creating Compressed Backups with tar

1. Create a compressed archive: `tar -czvf backup.tar.gz /path/to/directory`
2. Extract files from an archive: `tar -xzvf backup.tar.gz`

Introduction to Third-Party Backup Solutions

- **Duplicati:** User-friendly GUI for encrypted backups.
- **Timeshift:** Ideal for creating system snapshots.
- **Bacula:** Advanced tool for enterprise environments.

Tip: Choose tools based on your specific requirements, such as ease of use or scalability.

Recovering Lost Data

Understanding Data Recovery Scenarios

- Accidental file deletion.
- Corrupted or deleted partitions.
- Damaged storage devices.

Using testdisk for Partition Recovery

1. Install testdisk: `sudo apt install testdisk`
2. Run testdisk to analyze the disk: `sudo testdisk`
3. Follow the interactive menu to recover partitions.

Recovering Files with photorec

1. Install photorec (part of testdisk): `sudo apt install testdisk`
2. Launch photorec: `sudo photorec`
3. Select the disk and file type to recover.

Limitations of Data Recovery

- Data recovery may not be possible if the storage has been overwritten.
- Using professional services may be necessary for severe cases.

Warning: Avoid writing new data to the affected disk to maximize recovery chances.

Real-World Scenario:

- A user recovers photos accidentally deleted from an SD card using photorec.

Automating Backup Processes

Setting Up Cron Jobs for Automated Backups

1. Edit the crontab file: `crontab -e`
2. Add a job to back up daily: `0 2 * * * rsync -av /source/directory /backup/directory`

Monitoring Backup Tasks and Logs

- Redirect backup output to a log file: `rsync -av /source/directory /backup/directory >> /var/log/backup.log 2>&1`
- Review logs regularly: `cat /var/log/backup.log`

Tip: Automating backups ensures consistency and reduces manual effort.

Real-World Scenario:

- A server admin sets up a cron job to automate daily backups to a remote server and monitors logs weekly.

Cloud-Based Backup Solutions

Advantages of Cloud Backups

- Accessible from anywhere.
- Provides off-site storage for disaster recovery.
- Scalable storage options.

Popular Cloud Backup Services

- **Google Drive:** Integrates with Linux using rclone.
- **Dropbox:** Offers native Linux clients.
- **AWS S3:** Ideal for large-scale or enterprise backups.

Ensuring Security in Cloud Backups

- Encrypt data before uploading using tools like GPG: `gpg -c backup.tar.gz`
- Use strong passwords and enable two-factor authentication.

Warning: Unencrypted cloud backups may expose sensitive data. Always secure your backups.

Real-World Scenario:

- A small business uses AWS S3 with GPG encryption to store financial data securely in the cloud.

Restoring Backups

Testing Backup Restorations

- Regularly test restorations to ensure data integrity.
- Example: Extract files from a tar archive:
  `tar -xzvf backup.tar.gz -C /restore/path`

Restoring Files from Compressed Archives

- Restore specific files: `tar -xzvf backup.tar.gz /path/to/file`

Step-by-Step Guide for Recovering Systems from Backups

1. Boot from a live Linux environment.
2. Mount the backup drive: `sudo mount /dev/sdX /mnt`
3. Restore files to the target location using rsync: `rsync -av /mnt/backup/directory /target/directory`

4. Verify the restoration.

Tip: Document the restoration process for future reference.

Real-World Scenario:

- A server admin restores a production database from a nightly backup following a hardware failure.

Best Practices for Backup and Recovery

1. **Keep Multiple Backup Copies:** Use the 3-2-1 rule (3 copies, 2 local, 1 off-site).
2. **Encrypt Sensitive Data:** Protect backups with strong encryption.
3. **Test Regularly:** Verify backups and restorations periodically.
4. **Document Procedures:** Maintain clear instructions for backup and recovery.

Warning: Neglecting backups can result in irreversible data loss. Implement robust backup strategies immediately.

Summary This chapter covered the essentials of backups and data recovery, including strategies, tools, and best practices. By automating processes and testing restorations, you can safeguard critical data and ensure system resiliency.

Chapter 16: Securing Your Linux System

Overview System security is a critical aspect of Linux administration. A secure system protects sensitive data, ensures uninterrupted operations, and mitigates the risk of unauthorized access or cyberattacks. This chapter covers essential security practices, tools, and techniques to enhance the protection of Linux systems.

By the end of this chapter, you will:

- Understand the importance of system security.
- Learn to configure firewalls and secure authentication.
- Monitor and log system activities for security purposes.
- Implement best practices for system security.

Importance of System Security

Why Security is Critical in Linux Systems

- Protects sensitive data from breaches and theft.
- Ensures system stability by preventing malicious activities.
- Complies with legal and regulatory requirements.

Common Threats to Linux Environments

- **Unauthorized Access:** Weak passwords or unprotected services.
- **Malware and Rootkits:** Malicious software targeting Linux systems.
- **Denial of Service (DoS) Attacks:** Overloading system resources.
- **Exploited Vulnerabilities:** Unpatched software or misconfigurations.

Note: A multi-layered security approach significantly reduces risks.

Real-World Scenario:

- A company mitigates ransomware threats by enforcing secure authentication, using regular updates, and implementing robust backup policies.

Configuring Firewalls

What is a Firewall? A firewall is a security tool that filters incoming and outgoing network traffic based on predefined rules, protecting the system from unauthorized access.

Using ufw (Uncomplicated Firewall) for Basic Configuration

1. Enable ufw:
   ```
   sudo ufw enable
   ```
2. Allow specific services:
   ```
   sudo ufw allow ssh
   sudo ufw allow 80/tcp
   ```
3. Check firewall status:
   ```
   sudo ufw status
   ```

Advanced Firewall Rules with iptables

1. Install iptables (if not already installed):
   ```
   sudo apt install iptables
   ```
2. Block a specific IP address:
   ```
   sudo iptables -A INPUT -s 192.168.1.100 -j DROP
   ```
3. Save iptables rules:
   ```
   sudo iptables-save > /etc/iptables/rules.v4
   ```

Comparison of ufw and iptables

Feature	ufw	iptables
Ease of Use	Simple, beginner-friendly interface	Advanced, requires detailed syntax
Use Case	Basic firewall configurations	Complex and granular rules
Logging	Limited	Extensive

Warning: Improper firewall configurations can block legitimate traffic. Test rules carefully.

Keeping Your System Updated

Importance of Regular Updates

- Patches vulnerabilities in software.
- Ensures compatibility with the latest features.
- Protects against newly discovered threats.

Using Package Managers for Security Patches

- Update packages on Debian-based systems: `sudo apt update && sudo apt upgrade`
- Update packages on Red Hat-based systems: `sudo yum update`

Automating Updates with Cron

1. Create a cron job for automatic updates:
   ```
   sudo crontab -e
   ```
2. Add the following line for daily updates:
   ```
   0 3 * * * apt update && apt upgrade -y
   ```

Real-World Scenario:

- A server admin schedules daily updates using cron jobs to ensure critical vulnerabilities are patched promptly.

Tip: Enable automatic notifications to stay informed about updates.

Implementing Secure Authentication

Enforcing Strong Password Policies

- Edit /etc/security/pwquality.conf to set password complexity requirements:
  ```
  minlen = 12
  minclass = 3
  ```
- Use chage to enforce password expiration:
  ```
  sudo chage -M 90 username
  ```

Configuring Two-Factor Authentication (2FA)

1. Install Google Authenticator:
   ```
   sudo apt install libpam-google-authenticator
   ```
2. Set up 2FA for a user:
   ```
   google-authenticator
   ```
3. Edit PAM configuration to require 2FA:
   ```
   sudo nano /etc/pam.d/sshd
   ```
   Add: auth required pam_google_authenticator.so

Using SSH Key-Based Authentication

1. Generate SSH keys:
   ```
   ssh-keygen -t rsa -b 4096
   ```
2. Copy the public key to the server:
   ```
   ssh-copy-id user@server_ip
   ```
3. Disable password authentication in
   /etc/ssh/sshd_config: PasswordAuthentication no
   Restart SSH: sudo systemctl restart ssh

Comparison of Authentication Methods

Method	Security Level	Ease of Implementation	Use Case
Passwords	Moderate (if strong)	Simple	Basic systems
2FA	High	Requires configuration	Secure remote access
SSH Keys	Very High	Requires setup	Server and admin accounts

Tip: Combine 2FA with SSH key authentication for maximum security.

Using SELinux and AppArmor

Overview of SELinux (Security-Enhanced Linux) SELinux provides mandatory access control (MAC) policies to secure Linux systems.

Configuring SELinux Modes

- Check current mode: `getenforce`
- Change mode to enforcing: `sudo setenforce 1`
- Persist mode changes in `/etc/selinux/config`.

Introduction to AppArmor for Application Security

- Check AppArmor status: `sudo apparmor_status`
- Enable profiles for an application: `sudo aa-enforce /path/to/profile`

Comparison of SELinux and AppArmor

Feature	SELinux	AppArmor
Security Model	Mandatory Access Control (MAC)	Profile-Based Access Control
Configuration	Complex	Simpler, file-based profiles
Use Case	Enterprise environments	Lightweight systems or desktops

Warning: Improper configurations can block legitimate operations. Test policies in permissive mode first.

Monitoring and Logging for Security
Importance of Monitoring System Logs
- Identifies unusual or malicious activities.
- Helps in troubleshooting security incidents.

Tools for Log Analysis
- Use `journalctl` for system logs: `journalctl -xe`
- Analyze logs with `logwatch`: `sudo apt install logwatch logwatch`

Setting Up Intrusion Detection Systems (IDS)
- Install AIDE (Advanced Intrusion Detection Environment):
  ```
  sudo apt install aide
  sudo aideinit
  ```
- Verify changes: `sudo aide --check`

Real-World Scenario:
- An organization uses AIDE to monitor critical system files for unauthorized changes.

Tip: Regular log analysis helps detect potential threats early.

Securing Network Services
Disabling Unnecessary Services
- List active services:
  ```
  sudo systemctl list-units --type=service
  ```
- Disable unwanted services:
  ```
  sudo systemctl disable servicename
  ```

Configuring Secure Communication Protocols
- Install and configure HTTPS with Let's Encrypt:
  ```
  sudo apt install certbot python3-certbot-nginx
  sudo certbot --nginx
  ```
- Use SFTP instead of FTP for secure file transfers.

Setting Up Fail2Ban to Prevent Brute-Force Attacks
1. Install Fail2Ban: `sudo apt install fail2ban`
2. Configure jail settings:
   ```
   sudo nano /etc/fail2ban/jail.local
   ```
3. Restart Fail2Ban: `sudo systemctl restart fail2ban`

Warning: Regularly review Fail2Ban logs to ensure legitimate users are not blocked.

Backup and Recovery for Security
Best Practices for Secure Backups
- Use encryption tools like GPG for sensitive data:
  ```
  gpg -c backup.tar.gz
  ```
- Store backups in multiple secure locations (local and off-site).

Testing Backup Integrity and Recovery Plans
- Regularly restore backups to verify integrity.
- Document recovery procedures for quick access during incidents.

Tip: Secure backups protect against data breaches and ransomware attacks.

Best Practices for Linux Security
1. **Regularly Review Security Policies:** Update policies to adapt to emerging threats.
2. **Conduct Penetration Testing:** Identify vulnerabilities before attackers exploit them.
3. **Stay Updated:** Follow security news and apply updates promptly.
4. **Minimize Attack Surface:** Disable unnecessary services and close unused ports.
5. **Educate Users:** Train users on secure practices like recognizing phishing attempts.

Summary This chapter covered essential practices and tools for securing Linux systems. By implementing firewalls, securing authentication, monitoring logs, and staying updated, you can create a robust security framework that minimizes risks and ensures system integrity.

Chapter 17: Advanced Command-Line Tools

Overview of Advanced Command-Line Tools The command line is a powerful interface that provides flexibility, automation, and efficiency for managing Linux systems. This chapter explores advanced command-line tools that simplify complex tasks, automate processes, and troubleshoot issues effectively.

By the end of this chapter, you will:

- Master advanced text-processing tools like grep, awk, and sed.
- Use find and xargs for efficient file searching and processing.
- Automate file management with rsync.
- Debug and monitor applications with strace and lsof.
- Combine tools for advanced automation and problem-solving.

Importance of Mastering the Command Line

- Enables precise and efficient control over system operations.
- Facilitates automation of repetitive tasks.
- Provides tools for effective troubleshooting and debugging.

Key Tools for Efficiency and Automation

- **grep:** Searches text patterns in files.
- **awk:** Processes and formats text data.
- **sed:** Edits streams of text.
- **find:** Locates files and directories.
- **xargs:** Builds pipelines for efficient data handling.
- **rsync:** Synchronizes files and directories.
- **strace and lsof:** Debugging and monitoring tools.

Using grep for Pattern Matching

Basics of grep Syntax

- Syntax: `grep [options] pattern [file...]`

Examples: Searching for Text in Files

1. Search for a specific word in a file
   ```
   grep "error" /var/log/syslog
   ```
2. Perform a case-insensitive search:
   ```
   grep -i "warning" /var/log/syslog
   ```

Using Regular Expressions with grep
- Match lines starting with "root":
  ```
  grep "^root" /etc/passwd
  ```
- Search for lines ending with ".log":
  ```
  grep "\.log$" filelist.txt
  ```

Advanced Options
- Count matching lines: `grep -c "error" /var/log/syslog`
- Display line numbers: `grep -n "error" /var/log/syslog`

Comparison of grep, awk, and sed

Tool	Primary Use	Example Command
grep	Searching patterns in files	`grep "error" /var/log/syslog`
awk	Formatting and processing	`awk '{print $1, $2}' file.txt`
sed	Stream editing	`sed 's/foo/bar/g' file.txt`

Mastering awk for Text Processing

What is awk and Why Use It? awk is a versatile text-processing tool that extracts, manipulates, and formats data from files or streams.

Manipulating and Filtering Data
- Print specific columns from a file: `awk '{print $1, $3}' data.txt`
- Filter rows based on conditions: `awk '$2 > 100 {print $1, $2}' sales.txt`

Advanced awk Features
- Print lines matching a condition: `awk '/pattern/ {print $0}' file.txt`
- Replace a specific field in a file: `awk '{$2="NEW"; print}' file.txt`

Writing Simple awk Programs
1. Calculate the sum of a column: `awk '{sum += $2} END {print sum}' numbers.txt`
2. Count the number of lines in a file: `awk 'END {print NR}' file.txt`

Tip: Combine awk with other tools like grep for more advanced operations.

Simplifying Tasks with sed

Introduction to Stream Editing sed processes and edits text streams in real-time.

Substituting Text in Files

- Replace "foo" with "bar": `sed 's/foo/bar/' file.txt`
- Replace all occurrences in a file: `sed -i 's/foo/bar/g' file.txt`

Practical Examples of sed Commands

1. Delete empty lines: `sed '/^$/d' file.txt`
2. Append text after a match: `sed '/pattern/a\New line of text' file.txt`
3. Extract specific lines: `sed -n '10,20p' file.txt`

Warning: Use `-i` carefully as it modifies files in place.

Working with find for File Search

Locating Files and Directories

- Find files by name: `find /path -name "filename"`
- Search for directories: `find /path -type d -name "dirname"`

Combining find with Other Commands

- Remove files older than 7 days: `find /path -type f -mtime +7 -exec rm {} \;`
- List files larger than 1GB: `find /path -type f -size +1G`

Advanced find Features (size, type, permissions)

- Search for files with specific permissions: `find /path -perm 644`
- Find files owned by a specific user: `find /path -user username`

Tip: Use `find` with `-exec` or `xargs` for powerful automation.

xargs: Building Command Pipelines

What is xargs? `xargs` builds and executes command pipelines with arguments supplied by other commands.

Combining xargs with find, grep, and Other Tools

- Delete files found by find: `find /path -name "*.tmp" | xargs rm`
- Search for a pattern in multiple files: `find /path -name "*.log" | xargs grep "error"`

Advanced xargs Features

- Execute commands in parallel:
  ```
  find /path -name "*.txt" | xargs -P 4 gzip
  ```
- Limit the number of arguments per command:
  ```
  find /path -name "*.txt" | xargs -n 5 rm
  ```

Tip: Use xargs -P for parallel execution to improve performance.

Powerful File Management with rsync

Synchronizing Directories Locally and Remotely

- Sync directories locally: rsync -av /source/ /destination/
- Sync directories over SSH: rsync -avz /source/ user@remote_host:/destination/

Common rsync Options and Flags

- -a: Archive mode (preserves permissions, timestamps, etc.).
- -v: Verbose output.
- -z: Enable compression during transfer.
- --delete: Remove files from the destination that no longer exist in the source.

Automating Backups with rsync

- Schedule rsync with cron: crontab -e
  Add: 0 2 * * * rsync -av /source/ /destination/

Tip: Always test rsync commands with the --dry-run option before execution.

Command Chaining and Redirection

Using Pipes (|) to Combine Commands

- Pass output from one command to another: ps aux | grep "apache"

Redirecting Input and Output (>, >>, <)

- Redirect output to a file: ls > filelist.txt
- Append output to a file: echo "New Line" >> filelist.txt

Chaining Commands with && and ||

- Execute commands conditionally: mkdir newdir && cd newdir
  - If mkdir fails, cd won't execute.

Tip: Use pipes and redirection to create complex workflows efficiently.

Debugging and Monitoring with strace and lsof

Introduction to strace for System Calls Debugging

- Trace system calls made by a command: `strace ls`
- Debug application startup issues: `strace -e open application`

Monitoring Open Files with lsof

- List files opened by a specific process: `lsof -p PID`
- Find which process is using a port: `lsof -i :80`

Practical Examples for Debugging Applications

- Trace failed file access: `strace -e open application 2>&1 | grep "No such file"`
- Identify resource usage: `lsof +D /path/to/directory`

Tip: Combine `strace` and `lsof` with logging for detailed troubleshooting.

Practical Scenarios and Use Cases

Solving Real-World Problems with Command-Line Tools

- Example: Automating log file analysis:
  `grep "ERROR" /var/log/syslog | awk '{print $1, $2, $3}' > error_report.txt`
- Example: Backing up configuration files:
  `rsync -av /etc/ /backup/etc/`

Combining Tools for Advanced Automation

- Example: Find and archive old log files: `find /var/log -type f -mtime +30 | xargs tar -czvf old_logs.tar.gz`

Summary Advanced command-line tools empower Linux users to perform complex tasks efficiently. By mastering tools like grep, awk, sed, find, rsync, and strace, you can automate workflows, troubleshoot issues, and manage systems effectively.

Chapter 18: Linux Networking Services

Introduction to Networking in Linux Networking is a fundamental aspect of any Linux system, enabling communication between devices, servers, and the internet. Linux offers powerful networking tools and services that make it a preferred choice in various networking environments, from personal setups to enterprise systems.

By the end of this chapter, you will:

- Understand essential networking concepts and Linux's role in networking.
- Configure and manage network settings and services effectively.
- Troubleshoot and optimize network performance using Linux tools.

Basics of Networking Concepts

- **Networking Fundamentals:** Refers to the exchange of data between devices using communication protocols like TCP/IP.
- **Linux in Networking:** Frequently used as a router, firewall, server, or load balancer due to its flexibility and robust tools.
- **Key Networking Terms:**
    - **IP Address:** Identifies a device on a network.
    - **Subnet Mask:** Defines network boundaries.
    - **Gateway:** Facilitates communication between networks.
    - **DNS:** Resolves domain names to IP addresses.

The Role of Linux in Networking Environments

- Provides robust tools for managing servers, firewalls, and advanced networking configurations.
- Forms the foundation of many modern networking technologies, such as VPNs, load balancing, and software-defined networking (SDN).

Understanding Network Configuration

Static vs. Dynamic IP Addressing

- **Static IP:** Manually assigned and does not change.
    - Example: Servers often use static IPs for reliability and consistent access.

- **Dynamic IP:** Assigned automatically by DHCP.
  - Example: Client devices like laptops and mobile phones commonly use dynamic IPs.

Configuring Network Interfaces

- Use **ifconfig** (deprecated in some distributions) or **ip** (the modern preferred tool) for network interface management.

Configuring an Interface with ip:

1. Assign an IP address: `sudo ip addr add 192.168.1.10/24 dev eth0`
2. Bring the interface up: `sudo ip link set eth0 up`
3. Verify the configuration: `ip addr show eth0`

Tools for Managing Network Settings

- **ifconfig:** Legacy tool for managing network interfaces.
- **ip:** Modern and versatile tool for configuring and monitoring network settings.
- **nmcli:** A command-line interface for managing NetworkManager, useful for complex network setups.

nmcli Examples:

- Show all connections: `nmcli connection show`
- Configure a static IP: `nmcli connection modify "Wired connection 1" ipv4.addresses 192.168.1.10/24 ipv4.gateway 192.168.1.1 ipv4.method manual`
- Restart the connection: `nmcli connection up "Wired connection 1"`

DNS and DHCP in Linux

What is DNS and How It Works

- DNS translates human-readable domain names (e.g., www.example.com) into machine-readable IP addresses.
- **DNS Workflow:** A user query is sent to a DNS resolver, which retrieves the IP address from an authoritative DNS server.

Configuring a DNS Server

1. Install BIND (a popular DNS server): `sudo apt install bind9`
2. Edit the configuration file: `sudo nano /etc/bind/named.conf.local`
   Add zone information: `zone "example.com" {`
   ```
       type master;
       file "/etc/bind/db.example.com";
   };
   ```
3. Restart the DNS server: `sudo systemctl restart bind9`

Understanding and Setting Up DHCP

- **DHCP:** Dynamically assigns IP addresses and network configurations to devices on the network.
- Install a DHCP server: `sudo apt install isc-dhcp-server`
- Configure DHCP ranges in `/etc/dhcp/dhcpd.conf`: `subnet 192.168.1.0 netmask 255.255.255.0 {`
  ```
      range 192.168.1.100 192.168.1.200;
      option routers 192.168.1.1;
      option domain-name-servers 8.8.8.8;
  }
  ```
- Start the service: `sudo systemctl start isc-dhcp-server`

Tip: Regularly test DNS and DHCP configurations to ensure correct operation.

Setting Up Proxy Servers

Basics of Proxy Servers

- Proxies act as intermediaries between clients and servers, enhancing security, privacy, and performance.

Configuring Squid Proxy

1. Install Squid:
   `sudo apt install squid`
2. Edit the Squid configuration file:
   `sudo nano /etc/squid/squid.conf`
   Add: `acl allowed_ips src 192.168.1.0/24`
   `http_access allow allowed_ips`
3. Restart Squid: `sudo systemctl restart squid`

Benefits and Use Cases of Proxies

- Improves performance through caching frequently accessed resources.
- Enhances network security by filtering content and restricting access.
- Provides anonymity by masking client IP addresses.

Linux Firewall Configuration

Overview of iptables and firewalld

- **iptables:** A powerful, low-level tool for creating and managing firewall rules.
- **firewalld:** A higher-level tool that simplifies managing iptables rules using zones and services.

Creating Basic Rules with iptables

- Allow SSH traffic:
  ```
  sudo iptables -A INPUT -p tcp --dport 22 -j ACCEPT
  ```
- Block a specific IP address:
  ```
  sudo iptables -A INPUT -s 192.168.1.100 -j DROP
  ```

Configuring firewalld Zones and Services

1. List active zones:
   ```
   sudo firewall-cmd --get-active-zones
   ```
2. Allow HTTP traffic:
   ```
   sudo firewall-cmd --zone=public --add-service=http --permanent
   sudo firewall-cmd --reload
   ```

Comparison of iptables and firewalld

Feature	iptables	firewalld
Complexity	Requires detailed rule creation	Simplified with zones and services
Ideal Use Case	Granular control for advanced users	Quick setup for common use cases

Network File Sharing

Introduction to NFS (Network File System)

- NFS allows Linux systems to share directories and files over a network.

Setting Up and Managing NFS Shares

1. Install the NFS server: `sudo apt install nfs-kernel-server`
2. Configure shared directories in `/etc/exports`:
   `/shared_directory`
   `192.168.1.0/24(rw,sync,no_subtree_check)`
3. Restart the NFS server: `sudo systemctl restart nfs-kernel-server`

Samba for Cross-Platform File Sharing

- Samba enables file sharing between Linux and Windows systems.
- Install Samba: `sudo apt install samba`
- Configure shared directories in `/etc/samba/smb.conf`:
  `[shared]`
  `path = /shared_directory`
  `read only = no`
  `browsable = yes`
- Restart Samba: `sudo systemctl restart smbd`

Tip: Set appropriate permissions on shared directories for secure access.

Troubleshooting Networking Issues

Using Tools like ping, traceroute, and netstat

- **ping:** Tests connectivity to a host: `ping google.com`
- **traceroute:** Tracks the path packets take to a destination: `traceroute google.com`
- **netstat:** Displays active network connections: `netstat -tuln`

Analyzing and Debugging Connectivity Problems

- Check the status of network interfaces: `ip link show`
- Verify DNS resolution: `nslookup google.com`

Resolving DNS and IP Conflicts

- Restart the network service: `sudo systemctl restart networking`
- Release and renew IP addresses: `sudo dhclient -r`
  `sudo dhclient`

Performance Optimization for Networking

Understanding Network Bandwidth and Latency

- **Bandwidth:** Refers to the amount of data transferred over a network.
- **Latency:** Measures the delay in data transmission.

Tools for Monitoring Network Performance

- **iftop:** Monitors real-time bandwidth usage.
- **nload:** Visualizes incoming and outgoing network traffic.
- **iperf:** Tests network throughput between devices.

Summary This chapter provided a comprehensive overview of Linux networking services. By mastering these tools and configurations, you can set up robust networks, optimize performance, and resolve connectivity issues effectively.

Chapter 19: Managing Large File Systems

Introduction to Managing Large File Systems

As file systems grow in size and complexity, effective management becomes critical to ensure optimal performance and reliability. Linux provides a wide range of tools and techniques for managing large file systems, from partitioning and monitoring to advanced features like Logical Volume Management (LVM) and file system snapshots.

By the end of this chapter, you will:
- Understand the basics of file systems and their types.
- Learn to partition, format, and resize file systems.
- Explore tools for monitoring and maintaining file system health.

Understanding File Systems
What is a File System?
- A file system organizes and stores data on storage devices like hard drives, SSDs, and USB drives.
- It defines how files are named, accessed, and stored.

Types of File Systems
- **ext4:** The default file system for most Linux distributions; offers journaling and high reliability.
- **XFS:** A high-performance journaling file system suitable for large-scale systems.
- **NTFS:** Commonly used on Windows; supported in Linux with read/write access via tools like ntfs-3g.
- **FAT32/exFAT:** Ideal for USB drives and cross-platform compatibility.
- **Btrfs:** A modern file system with support for snapshots, compression, and scalability.
- **ZFS:** Designed for enterprise storage, offering redundancy, snapshots, and error correction.

File System	Key Features	Best Use Case
ext4	Journaling, reliability	General-purpose Linux systems
XFS	High performance	Large-scale or enterprise storage
NTFS	Windows compatibility	Dual-boot systems
FAT32/exFAT	Cross-platform compatibility	USB drives, external storage
Btrfs	Snapshots, compression, scalability	Advanced Linux systems
ZFS	Redundancy, snapshots, error correction	Enterprise and large-scale storage

Introduction to Logical Volume Management (LVM)

What is LVM?

- LVM is a storage management solution that allows flexible partitioning and resizing of disk space.
- It abstracts physical storage devices into logical volumes, enabling advanced features like snapshots and resizing.

Benefits of Using LVM

- **Flexibility:** Resize volumes without unmounting them.
- **Snapshots:** Create backups at a specific point in time.
- **Efficiency:** Combine multiple disks into a single volume group.

Practical Example of LVM Setup:

1. Create a physical volume: `sudo pvcreate /dev/sda1`
2. Create a volume group: `sudo vgcreate my_vg /dev/sda1`
3. Create a logical volume: `sudo lvcreate -L 20G -n my_lv my_vg`
4. Format and mount the logical volume: `sudo mkfs.ext4 /dev/my_vg/my_lv`
   `sudo mount /dev/my_vg/my_lv /mnt`

Partitioning for Large File Systems
Tools for Partitioning

- **fdisk:** Command-line utility for creating and managing partitions on MBR disks.
- **parted:** Supports GPT disks and provides advanced features.
- **gparted:** A graphical interface for partitioning tasks.

Practical Example: Setting Up a New Disk

1. **Identify the Disk:** List all available disks to identify the new one: `sudo fdisk -1`
2. **Partition the Disk:** Launch `fdisk` for the new disk (e.g., /dev/sdb): `sudo fdisk /dev/sdb`
   a. Press n to create a new partition.
   b. Specify the partition size and type.
   c. Press w to write changes to the disk.
3. **Format the Partition:** Format the newly created partition (e.g., /dev/sdb1) with a suitable file system: `sudo mkfs.ext4 /dev/sdb1`
4. **Create a Mount Point:** Make a directory to serve as the mount point: `sudo mkdir /mnt/newdisk`
5. **Mount the Partition:** Mount the formatted partition to the mount point: `sudo mount /dev/sdb1 /mnt/newdisk`
6. **Verify the Mount:** Check the mounted file system: `df -h`
7. **Make the Mount Persistent:** Edit the /etc/fstab file to ensure the disk mounts automatically: `sudo nano /etc/fstab`
   Add an entry: `/dev/sdb1 /mnt/newdisk ext4 defaults 0 0`
   Test the configuration: `sudo mount -a`

Comparison of Partitioning Tools

Tool	Key Features	Best Use Case
fdisk	CLI, MBR support	Simple setups
parted	CLI, GPT support	Advanced or large disks
gparted	GUI, versatile options	User-friendly partitioning

Managing Disk Space Efficiently

Monitoring Disk Usage

- **df:** Displays disk usage statistics: `df -h`
- **du:** Analyzes directory sizes: `du -sh /path/to/directory`

Cleaning Up Unused Files

- Identify large files: `find / -type f -size +1G`
- Clear temporary files: `sudo rm -rf /tmp/*`

Tip: Automate cleanup tasks using cron jobs.

Expanding and Shrinking File Systems

Resizing Logical Volumes Safely

- **Expand a Logical Volume:**
  - ○ Extend the logical volume: `sudo lvextend -L +10G /dev/my_vg/my_lv`
  - ○ Resize the file system: `sudo resize2fs /dev/my_vg/my_lv`
- **Shrink a Logical Volume:**
  - ○ Unmount the volume: `sudo umount /dev/my_vg/my_lv`
  - ○ Resize the file system: `sudo resize2fs /dev/my_vg/my_lv 15G`
  - ○ Reduce the logical volume: `sudo lvreduce -L 15G /dev/my_vg/my_lv`

Using resize2fs and Other Tools

- `resize2fs` works for ext-based file systems.
- For XFS file systems, use: `sudo xfs_growfs /mount/point`

File System Integrity and Maintenance

Checking File System Health with fsck

- Check and repair file systems: `sudo fsck /dev/sda1`

Repairing File System Errors

- Automatically fix errors: `sudo fsck -y /dev/sda1`

Tip: Schedule regular checks for critical file systems.

Mounting and Unmounting File Systems

Understanding Mount Points

- A mount point is a directory where a file system is accessed.
- Example: `sudo mount /dev/sda1 /mnt`

Configuring /etc/fstab for Persistent Mounts

1. Edit the `/etc/fstab` file: `sudo nano /etc/fstab`
2. Add an entry: `/dev/sda1 /mnt ext4 defaults 0 0`
3. Test the configuration: `sudo mount -a`

Advanced File System Features

Snapshots with LVM

- Create a snapshot: `sudo lvcreate -L 5G -s -n my_snapshot /dev/my_vg/my_lv`
- Use snapshots for backups or testing without affecting the original data.

Journaling and Its Benefits

- Journaling minimizes data corruption by recording metadata changes before they are applied.
- File systems like ext4 and XFS support journaling.

Introduction to RAID

- RAID provides redundancy and performance improvement by combining multiple disks.
- Types include RAID 0 (striping), RAID 1 (mirroring), and RAID 5 (striping with parity).
- Create a RAID array using `mdadm`: `sudo mdadm --create --verbose /dev/md0 --level=1 --raid-devices=2 /dev/sda /dev/sdb`

Best Practices for Managing Large File Systems

Backup Strategies for Critical Data

- Use `rsync` for efficient backups: `rsync -av /source/ /backup/`
- Automate backups using cron jobs or systemd timers.

Periodic Maintenance and Monitoring

- Schedule regular checks with `fsck`.
- Monitor disk health with SMART tools: `sudo smartctl -a /dev/sda`

Chapter 20: Automating Tasks with Cron and Systemd

Introduction to Automation in Linux Automation plays a crucial role in simplifying repetitive tasks, ensuring system reliability, and reducing manual intervention. Linux provides powerful tools like Cron and Systemd for scheduling and automating tasks effectively.

By the end of this chapter, you will:
- Understand the importance of task automation in Linux.
- Learn to schedule tasks using Cron and Systemd.
- Troubleshoot and optimize automation workflows.

Importance of Automation in System Administration
- **Efficiency:** Automates repetitive tasks like backups, updates, and monitoring.
- **Consistency:** Ensures tasks are performed at regular intervals without errors.
- **Scalability:** Enables administrators to manage large systems efficiently.

Common Use Cases for Task Scheduling
- Scheduling regular backups.
- Performing system updates.
- Cleaning up temporary files.
- Monitoring and logging system metrics.

Understanding Cron

What is Cron?
- Cron is a time-based task scheduler in Linux.
- It runs jobs (scripts or commands) at specified times or intervals.

Overview of Cron Jobs and Syntax
- Cron jobs are defined in a **crontab** file.
- Syntax: `minute hour day month day_of_week command`

Field	Accepted Values
Minute	0-59
Hour	0-23
Day of Month	1-31
Month	1-12 or Jan-Dec
Day of Week	0-6 (0 = Sunday) or Sun-Sat

Creating and Managing Cron Jobs

Writing Basic Cron Jobs

1. Open the crontab editor: `crontab -e`
2. Add a job: `0 2 * * * /usr/local/bin/backup.sh`
   a. Runs `backup.sh` at 2:00 AM daily.

Using Time Intervals for Scheduling

- Schedule a job every 5 minutes: `*/5 * * * * /path/to/script.sh`
- Run a task every Sunday at midnight: `0 0 * * 0 /path/to/task.sh`

Advanced Cron Features

Setting Up Email Notifications for Cron Jobs

- Add the following line to receive output via email: `MAILTO="user@example.com"`

Debugging Cron Jobs Using Logs

- Check the cron log for errors: `sudo grep CRON /var/log/syslog`

Restricting User Access to Cron

- Use `/etc/cron.allow` and `/etc/cron.deny` to manage user permissions.

Introduction to Systemd

What is Systemd?

- A modern system and service manager for Linux.
- Provides an alternative to Cron with enhanced features like dependency handling and parallel execution.

Comparison Between Cron and Systemd

Feature	Cron	Systemd
Simplicity	Easy to set up	Requires understanding unit files
Dependency Handling	Limited	Advanced
Logging	Minimal	Comprehensive
Use Cases	Simple periodic tasks	Complex tasks and dependencies

Creating and Managing Systemd Units

Understanding Unit Files and Their Structure

- Unit files define services, timers, and other tasks.
- Location: `/etc/systemd/system/`
- Basic structure: `[Unit]`
  `Description=Task description`

  `[Service]`
  `ExecStart=/path/to/command`

  `[Install]`
  `WantedBy=multi-user.target`

Creating a Systemd Timer Unit

1. Create a service file: `sudo nano /etc/systemd/system/example.service`
   Content: `[Unit]`
   `Description=Example Task`

   `[Service]`
   `ExecStart=/path/to/script.sh`

2. Create a timer file: `sudo nano /etc/systemd/system/example.timer`
   Content: `[Unit]`
   `Description=Run Example Task Daily`

```
[Timer]
OnCalendar=*-*-* 02:00:00

[Install]
WantedBy=timers.target
```

3. Enable and start the timer: `sudo systemctl enable example.timer`
   `sudo systemctl start example.timer`

Managing Systemd Timers

- List all timers: `systemctl list-timers`
- Check the status of a timer: `systemctl status example.timer`

Practical Examples of Task Automation

Automating Backups Using Cron

- Example cron job to back up a directory daily: `0 1 * * * tar -czf /backup/$(date +\%F).tar.gz /important_data`

Setting Up System Maintenance Tasks with Systemd

- Use Systemd to clean temporary files weekly:
  - Create a script (`/usr/local/bin/clean_tmp.sh`):
    ```
    #!/bin/bash
    rm -rf /tmp/*
    ```
  - Create a service and timer as shown above.

Troubleshooting Automation Issues

Common Errors with Cron Jobs and Fixes

- **Issue:** Script doesn't execute.
  - **Solution:** Check file permissions and ensure it's executable: `chmod +x /path/to/script.sh`
- **Issue:** Environment variables not set.
  - **Solution:** Use absolute paths or source the environment in the script.

Debugging Systemd Timers

- View recent logs: `journalctl -u example.timer`
- Check for errors in the service unit: `systemctl status example.service`

Best Practices for Task Automation

Organizing and Documenting Scheduled Tasks

- Keep a log of all active cron jobs and timers for easy reference.
- Use descriptive names for scripts and timers.

Testing Automation Scripts in a Safe Environment

- Test scripts manually before scheduling them.
- Use a test server for complex automation setups.

Monitoring and Updating Task Schedules Regularly

- Periodically review and update schedules to match current requirements.
- Monitor task execution using logs and alerts.

Summary Automating tasks with Cron and Systemd can significantly enhance system administration by reducing manual effort and ensuring consistency. By understanding their features and best practices, you can effectively schedule, monitor, and troubleshoot tasks on Linux systems.

Chapter 21: Introduction to Linux Security

Introduction to Linux Security

Linux security is a cornerstone of modern computing, providing robust protection against threats while maintaining system performance. With Linux powering a significant portion of servers, desktops, and embedded devices, understanding its security mechanisms is critical for users and administrators alike.

By the end of this chapter, you will:

- Understand the importance of Linux security.
- Learn about common threats and built-in security features.
- Explore best practices and practical scenarios to enhance security.

What is Linux Security?

Definition and Importance

- **Definition:** Linux security encompasses tools, practices, and configurations designed to protect systems from unauthorized access, vulnerabilities, and data breaches.
- **Importance:** Ensures system integrity, protects sensitive data, and mitigates threats in today's interconnected world.

The Role of Security in Modern Systems

- Safeguards against evolving threats, including malware, unauthorized access, and zero-day exploits.
- Enhances trust and reliability in systems handling critical workloads or sensitive information.

Common Security Threats

Malware and Viruses

- While less common on Linux than other platforms, threats like rootkits and ransomware can target Linux systems.
- **Examples:** The "Dirty Pipe" exploit leveraged to escalate privileges.

Unauthorized Access

- Weak passwords or improperly configured remote access can expose systems to unauthorized users.

Exploits and Vulnerabilities

- Software bugs and outdated packages may be exploited to gain unauthorized privileges or execute malicious code.
- **Example:** Leaving default configurations unchanged can lead to system compromises.

Security Features of Linux

Built-in Security Mechanisms

- **User and Group-Based Permissions:** Controls access to files and directories based on ownership and permissions.
- **File Permissions:** Defines read (r), write (w), and execute (x) access for users, groups, and others.
- **Example:** chmod 750 file.txt
- **Special Permission Modes:** Utilize setuid, setgid, and sticky bit for specific scenarios requiring advanced control.

Secure Shell (SSH) for Remote Access

- Encrypts remote communication to prevent eavesdropping.
- Configure key-based authentication for enhanced security:
  - Generate an SSH key pair: ssh-keygen -t rsa
  - Copy the public key to the server: ssh-copy-id user@server
- **Additional Security Tip:** Restrict SSH access to specific IP ranges in /etc/hosts.allow and /etc/hosts.deny.

Data Encryption

- Encrypt sensitive data using tools like LUKS for disk encryption:
  - Initialize encryption: sudo cryptsetup luksFormat /dev/sdb1
  - Open the encrypted partition: sudo cryptsetup open /dev/sdb1 encrypted_disk
  - Mount the partition after formatting: sudo mkfs.ext4 /dev/mapper/encrypted_disk
    sudo mount /dev/mapper/encrypted_disk /mnt

- Use gpg to encrypt individual files: gpg -c file.txt

Keeping Your System Updated

Importance of Updates and Patches

- Regular updates fix known vulnerabilities and improve overall system security.
- **Note:** Many exploits leverage outdated software.

Automating Updates for Security

- Use tools like unattended-upgrades to automate updates:
  `sudo apt install unattended-upgrades`
  `sudo dpkg-reconfigure unattended-upgrades`

Configuring Firewalls

Understanding Firewalls in Linux

- A firewall filters incoming and outgoing traffic based on defined rules.
- Essential for preventing unauthorized access and mitigating attacks.

Basics of ufw (Uncomplicated Firewall)

- A user-friendly interface for managing firewall rules.
- Examples:
  - Allow SSH traffic: `sudo ufw allow ssh`
  - Enable the firewall: `sudo ufw enable`
  - Deny specific IPs: `sudo ufw deny from 192.168.1.100`

Using iptables for Advanced Firewall Rules

- A powerful tool for configuring network packet filtering.
- Example: Allow HTTP traffic: `sudo iptables -A INPUT -p tcp --dport 80 -j ACCEPT`
- Save iptables rules for persistence: `sudo iptables-save > /etc/iptables/rules.v4`

Introduction to SELinux and AppArmor
Overview of Mandatory Access Control (MAC)
- Provides additional security by defining and enforcing policies that restrict access based on the process's role and context.

Configuring and Managing SELinux
- Check the current mode: `sestatus`
- Change the mode (temporary): `sudo setenforce 0`
- Configure SELinux policies for applications using `semanage`: `sudo semanage port -a -t ssh_port_t -p tcp 2222`

Basics of AppArmor Profiles
- AppArmor restricts program capabilities using profiles.
- Enable AppArmor: `sudo systemctl enable apparmor` `sudo systemctl start apparmor`
- Manage profiles: `aa-status`
- Customize profiles: `sudo nano /etc/apparmor.d/usr.bin.sshd`

Monitoring and Logging
Importance of System Logs
- Logs provide insights into system activity and potential security issues.

Using journalctl for Security Logs
- View system logs: `journalctl`
- Filter logs by service: `journalctl -u sshd`

Monitoring Tools for Intrusion Detection
- **AIDE (Advanced Intrusion Detection Environment):** Detects unauthorized changes to files: `sudo aide --init`
- **Fail2Ban:** Protects against brute-force attacks: `sudo apt install fail2ban`
- **Snort:** A network intrusion detection system: `sudo apt install snort`
- **OSSEC:** Open-source intrusion detection system for monitoring log files and file integrity.

Best Practices for Linux Security
Strong Password Policies
- Use password managers to generate and store strong passwords.
- Enforce password policies: `sudo nano /etc/security/pwquality.conf`

Limiting Root Access
- Disable direct root login in `/etc/ssh/sshd_config`: `PermitRootLogin no`

Regular Audits and Security Checks
- Periodically review user accounts and file permissions.
- Use tools like `lynis` for comprehensive security audits: `sudo apt install lynis`
`sudo lynis audit system`

Securing File Systems
- Use mount options to limit executable files: `sudo mount -o noexec,nosuid,nodev /dev/sda1 /mnt`
- Ensure sensitive directories like `/tmp` have secure mount options.

Common Mistakes and How to Avoid Them
Default Configuration Pitfalls
- Ensure default services are configured securely (e.g., change default passwords).

Neglecting Security Updates
- Automate updates to prevent missing critical patches.

Overlooking File and Directory Permissions
- Regularly review and correct permissions for sensitive files.

Practical Scenarios in Linux Security
Securing a Web Server
- Use ufw to allow only necessary traffic (e.g., HTTP, HTTPS): `sudo ufw allow 80`
`sudo ufw allow 443`
- Enable SSL/TLS for secure communication using `certbot`: `sudo certbot --apache`

Setting Up a Secure File Transfer Protocol (SFTP)

- Restrict users to their home directories: `Match User sftpuser ChrootDirectory /home/sftpuser ForceCommand internal-sftp`

Implementing Two-Factor Authentication (2FA)

- Install and configure Google Authenticator: `sudo apt install libpam-google-authenticator google-authenticator`
- Update PAM configuration to require 2FA: `sudo nano /etc/pam.d/sshd`

Summary Linux security is a dynamic field that requires continuous learning and adaptation to emerging threats. By leveraging built-in tools, following best practices, and staying proactive, administrators can significantly enhance the security of their Linux systems.

Chapter 22: Linux in the Enterprise

Linux has become a critical component in enterprise environments due to its flexibility, stability, and cost-effectiveness. From powering servers and cloud platforms to managing network infrastructure and high-performance computing (HPC), Linux provides robust solutions tailored to enterprise needs.

By the end of this chapter, you will:

- Understand why Linux is popular in businesses.
- Explore key enterprise-grade Linux distributions.
- Learn about Linux's applications in servers, virtualization, and security.

The Role of Linux in Enterprise Environments

Why Linux is Popular in Businesses

- **Open Source Benefits:** Cost savings, transparency, and a collaborative development model.
- **Stability and Security:** Designed for long-term reliability with a strong focus on security.
- **Scalability:** Capable of handling workloads ranging from small startups to global enterprises.

Open Source Benefits for Enterprises

- **Cost Efficiency:** No licensing fees compared to proprietary systems.
- **Customizability:** Tailor systems to meet specific business needs.
- **Community Support:** Backed by a vast community and commercial vendors.

Enterprise-Grade Linux Distributions

Overview of Red Hat Enterprise Linux (RHEL)

- **Target Audience:** Enterprises requiring stability and long-term support.
- **Key Features:**
    - Certified for major hardware and software vendors.
    - Advanced security features, such as SELinux.
    - Access to Red Hat's support and ecosystem.

SUSE Linux Enterprise Server (SLES)

- **Target Audience:** Businesses needing high availability and advanced management tools.
- **Key Features:**
  - Integrated tools for managing containers and virtualization.
  - Optimized for SAP applications and HPC environments.

Ubuntu Server for Enterprises

- **Target Audience:** Enterprises seeking a user-friendly, flexible server solution.
- **Key Features:**
  - Long-Term Support (LTS) releases for stability.
  - Extensive cloud platform integration (e.g., AWS, Azure).

Server Applications and Use Cases

Hosting Web and Database Servers

- **Web Servers:** Apache, Nginx.
  - Example: `sudo apt install apache2`
    `sudo systemctl enable apache2`
- **Database Servers:** MySQL, PostgreSQL.
  - Example: `sudo apt install mysql-server`
    `sudo mysql_secure_installation`

Application Servers and Middleware

- Hosts enterprise applications with middleware like Tomcat, JBoss, and WildFly.

Linux in High-Performance Computing (HPC)

- Used in supercomputers and research facilities for its scalability and performance.
- Example Tools:
  - SLURM for job scheduling.
  - OpenMPI for distributed computing.

Linux for Virtualization and Cloud Integration

Using KVM and QEMU for Virtualization

- KVM (Kernel-based Virtual Machine): Turns Linux into a hypervisor.
- Example Setup: `sudo apt install qemu-kvm libvirt-daemon-system`
  `sudo systemctl start libvirtd`

Integrating with Cloud Platforms (AWS, Azure, OpenStack)

- Supports cloud-native tools like Terraform, Kubernetes, and Ansible for seamless integration.
- Example: Provisioning an instance using AWS CLI: `aws ec2 run-instances --image-id ami-12345678 --count 1 --instance-type t2.micro`

Linux for Network Infrastructure

Configuring Firewalls with iptables and nftables

- **iptables Example:** `sudo iptables -A INPUT -p tcp --dport 22 -j ACCEPT`
- **nftables Example:** `sudo nft add rule ip filter input tcp dport 22 accept`

Managing DHCP and DNS Servers

- **DHCP Example:** `sudo apt install isc-dhcp-server`
  `sudo nano /etc/dhcp/dhcpd.conf`
- **DNS Example (BIND):** `sudo apt install bind9`
  `sudo nano /etc/bind/named.conf.local`

Linux as a Router or Proxy Server

- Configure IP forwarding: `sudo sysctl -w net.ipv4.ip_forward=1`
- Use Squid for proxy services: `sudo apt install squid`

Security and Compliance

Hardening Linux Systems for Enterprise Security

- Regularly update and patch the system: `sudo apt update && sudo apt upgrade`
- Use tools like Lynis for security audits: `sudo lynis audit system`

Managing Security Updates and Patching

- Automate updates with unattended-upgrades: `sudo apt install unattended-upgrades`

Compliance Standards and Auditing Tools

- Tools like OpenSCAP help ensure compliance with industry standards (e.g., PCI-DSS, HIPAA). `sudo apt install openscap-utils`
  ```
  oscap xccdf eval --profile
  xccdf_org.ssgproject.content_profile_pci-dss
  /usr/share/xml/scap/ssg/content/ssg-ubuntu1804-
  ds.xml
  ```

Automation and Configuration Management

Using Ansible for Enterprise Automation

- Example Playbook:
  ```
  - name: Install and start Apache
    hosts: webservers
    tasks:
      - name: Install Apache
        apt:
          name: apache2
          state: present
      - name: Start Apache service
        service:
          name: apache2
          state: started
  ```

Puppet and Chef for Configuration Management

- Puppet: Declarative management of system configurations.
- Chef: Automates application deployment and infrastructure management.

Streamlining Operations with Shell Scripts

- Example Backup Script:
  ```
  #!/bin/bash
  tar -czf /backup/$(date +%F).tar.gz /data
  ```

Enterprise Storage Solutions

Network File Systems (NFS and Samba)

- NFS Example:
  ```
  sudo apt install nfs-kernel-server
  sudo nano /etc/exports
  ```
- Samba Example:
  ```
  sudo apt install samba
  sudo nano /etc/samba/smb.conf
  ```

Distributed Storage with GlusterFS and Ceph

- GlusterFS: Scalable networked storage.
  ```
  sudo apt install glusterfs-server
  ```
- Ceph: Distributed object storage.
  ```
  sudo apt install ceph
  ```

Backup and Disaster Recovery Strategies

- Use tools like `rsync` for backups: `rsync -av /source /backup`
- Test disaster recovery plans regularly.

Case Studies: Linux in Action

Real-Life Examples of Linux in Large-Scale Deployments

- Linux powers the majority of the top 500 supercomputers globally.
- Examples include Google's infrastructure and NASA's data centers.

Success Stories from Industry Leaders

- Facebook uses Linux to manage its vast data centers.
- Amazon relies on Linux for its AWS services.

Best Practices for Linux in Enterprises

Planning and Scaling Linux Infrastructure

- Conduct thorough capacity planning for current and future needs.
- Use monitoring tools like Prometheus and Grafana for insights.

Training and Certification for Enterprise Teams

- Encourage certifications like RHCSA (Red Hat Certified System Administrator) and LFCS (Linux Foundation Certified System Administrator)

Building a Linux-Centric DevOps Culture

- Use CI/CD pipelines with tools like Jenkins and GitLab.
- Embrace containerization with Docker and Kubernetes.